BRIGHT NOTES

SILAS MARNER AND MIDDLEMARCH BY GEORGE ELIOT

Intelligent Education

Nashville, Tennessee

BRIGHT NOTES: Silas Marner and Middlemarch
www.BrightNotes.com

No part of this publication may be used or reproduced in any manner whatsoever without written permission, except in the case of brief quotations in critical articles and reviews. For permissions, contact Influence Publishers http://www.influencepublishers.com.

ISBN: 978-1-645421-62-7 (Paperback)
ISBN: 978-1-645421-63-4 (eBook)

Published in accordance with the U.S. Copyright Office Orphan Works and Mass Digitization report of the register of copyrights, June 2015.

Originally published by Monarch Press.
Thomas A. Duff, 1964
2020 Edition published by Influence Publishers.

Interior design by Lapiz Digital Services. Cover Design by Thinkpen Designs.

Printed in the United States of America.

Library of Congress Cataloging-in-Publication Data forthcoming.
Names: Intelligent Education
Title: BRIGHT NOTES: Silas Marner and Middlemarch
Subject: STU004000 STUDY AIDS / Book Notes

CONTENTS

1) Introduction to George Eliot   1

2) Textual Analysis
    Part One: Chapter 1   11
    Part One: Chapter 2   20
    Part One: Chapter 3   24
    Part One: Chapter 4   29
    Part One: Chapter 5   32
    Part One: Chapter 6   34
    Part One: Chapter 7   36
    Part One: Chapter 8   39
    Part One: Chapter 9   43
    Part One: Chapter 10   46
    Part One: Chapter 11   51
    Part One: Chapter 12   56
    Part One: Chapter 13   59
    Part One: Chapter 14   62
    Part One: Chapter 15   67
    Part Two: Chapter 1   69
    Part Two: Chapter 2   77
    Part Two: Chapter 3   81
    Part Two: Chapter 4   85
    Part Two: Chapters 5 and 6   90

3)	Character Analyses	97
4)	Essay Questions and Answers	102
5)	Prelude	106
6)	Textual Analysis	
	Book 1: Miss Brooke; Chapters 1 - 12	108
	Book 2: Old and Young; Chapters 13 - 22	130
	Book 3: Waiting for Death; Chapters 23 - 33	146
	Book 4: Three Love Problems; Chapters 34 - 42	159
	Book 5: The Dead Hand; Chapters 43 - 53	169
	Book 6: The Widow and the Wife; Chapters 54 - 62	181
	Book 7: Two Temptations; Chapters 63 - 71	188
	Book 8: Sunset and Sunrise; Chapters 72 - Finale	195
7)	Character Analyses	206
8)	Critical Commentary	212
9)	Essay Questions and Answers	219
10)	Bibliography	225

INTRODUCTION TO GEORGE ELIOT

SOCIAL BACKGROUND

Revolution was the key word of nineteenth-century Europe. It was the age of industrial revolution, of scientific upheaval culminating in Charles Darwin's *Origin of Species*, of political transformations brought on by the appeals of nationalism, liberalism and-at length-socialism. Although it escaped the violence and bloodshed that attended the change in the Continent, Britain emerged triumphant from the Napoleonic wars, and faced a series of economic and social crises. These years, the years of maturity for George Eliot (1819-1880), and the period of the narrative in *Middlemarch,* saw indignant and ultimately successful protests against a political system which, even in its most democratic branch, the House of Commons, permitted less than one-sixth of the adult male population to vote.

NEED FOR REFORM

The great mass of English workers lived in appalling misery and degradation-there was much truth in Napoleon's remark that the British ruling classes treated the rabble like slaves. A typical skilled textile-worker received eighty shillings for a ninety-hour, six-day week. And those who were employed were the lucky ones. Hundreds of thousands of unemployed workers lived in abject poverty in the slums of "machine-age" cities like Birmingham and Leeds. Many of these were displaced farmers driven from their lands by the Enclosures Acts. Although successful in putting English agriculture on a more efficient basis, and perhaps necessary to feed a growing population, this legislation increased and already swollen labor market and aggravated the misery of the workers. Conditions in factory towns were intolerable, but the proponents of reform, such as the Scottish industrialist Robert Owen or the clergyman Charles Kingsley, encountered a cold hostility from the gentry, who took comfort in the dismal dogmas of classical economists like Thomas Malthus, David Ricardo, and others preaching the futility of any attempt to alleviate poverty.

REFORM BILLS

These were the five measures which liberalized representation in the House of Commons. Prior to the first, the Reform Bill of 1832, representation in Parliament was based on a system dating from Queen Elizabeth I's reign (1558-1603), which failed to allow for shifts in population or the formation of new classes of society which followed in the wake of the Industrial Revolution. Two major abuses of the restrictions upon the franchise were:

1. "Pocket boroughs": those voting districts which were under the control of either the crown or of a large landholder.

2. "Rotten boroughs": These in which population had declined and whose power had fallen under the control of narrow town oligarchies or local landowners.

Each "pocket" or "rotten" borough, however, sent two members to Parliament; yet the large manufacturing cities such as Manchester and Birmingham were unrepresented. Of the total British population in 1831, consisting of twenty-four million people, only four hundred thousand were eligible to vote. Widespread corruption and the sale of parliamentary seats flourished, until dissatisfaction led to government action.

REFORM BILL OF 1832

Enacted under the Whig administration of Lord Grey, this first of five reform bills (the others were in 1867, 1884, 1918, and 1928) was far from perfect, but certain positive measures had been taken to adjust the inequity of the franchise:

1. Seats were redistributed, an action which thereby improved the power of the larger cities and towns.

2. In the boroughs, any person who occupied premises with an annual value of ten pounds received the franchise.

3. In the counties, any leaseholder who occupied premises with an annual value of ten pounds received the franchise.

4. Voter registration and voting procedure were simplified.

With the passage of the first Reform Bill over eight hundred thousand Englishmen were finally permitted to vote.

CHARTISM

In English reform movements, "Chartism" is the name given to the period of 1838-1848. The Reform Bill of 1832 failed to extend the franchise to the poorer classes; this fact, and a widespread discontent with economic deprivation, brought about widespread approval, in 1838, of the "People's Charter." Written by William Lovett and Francis Place, the document advocated the following:

1. Universal manhood suffrage.

2. Voting by secret ballot.

3. Election of Parliament annually.

4. Removal of property qualifications for the House of Commons.

5. Payment of salary for members of the House of Commons.

6. Formation of equal voting districts.

The movement, which had the support of many trade unions, represented the first attempt by the English working classes to win political power. Although a number of parliamentary reforms were begun under the Chartist activities, its force died out because of civil strife between moderate and extremist factions within the movement.

RATIONALISM

In religion, rationalism is the philosophical view which believes as true only those tenets or religious belief which can be established by reason. Supernatural revelation and the mysteries of faith are generally denied. Although the orthodox positions of formal religious faiths are found to be unacceptable by rationalistic standards, many individual rationalists find a positive force, an "Unseen Divinity," operating in the world. Others, however, deny the existence of a supreme being, and consider the most worthy reward one can expect for leading a good life is the life itself, and the hope that future generations of mankind will profit from it.

LIFE

In 1857, a middle-aged English woman upon the advice of her husband assumed the pen name of George Eliot and began to publish fiction. Two of her most popular novels, *Silas Marner* and *Middlemarch,* are widely read today, and her reputation as a major chronicler of English village life has endured for over a century.

Mary Ann (or Marian) Evans was born on November 22, 1819, at South Farm, Nuneaton (near Coventry), in Warwickshire, England. Her father, like Caleb Garth in *Middlemarch,* was an estate manager for several squires. He had five children, three by an earlier marriage. Mary Ann attended good boarding schools and excelled in language study until she was forced to return to supervise the family upon the death of her mother and the marriage of her sister (at which time she changed her name from Mary Ann to Marian).

Her love for language, however, did not cease; she continued her studies of German and Italian and also began the study of Hebrew. When she was twenty-two, the family moved to Coventry; here Mary Ann met and was influenced by the anti-

Christian philosophy of Charles Hennell and Charles Bray and his wife. It was shortly thereafter that she renounced her Evangelical (Anglican) beliefs. Although she continued to respect the viewpoint of churchgoers, she remained a skeptic until her death. Her father (who had been distressed by his daughter's loss of faith) died in 1849. This was three years after Marian had published a translation of the erudite German work, *The Life of Jesus* (Das Leben Jesu), an unorthodox view of Christ which denied the supernatural elements in the Gospels.

After her father's death, she went abroad for eighteen months, returning home in 1851 to accept a post as assistant editor with *The Westminster Review*. Living in the London building which housed the magazine offices, she soon became immersed in a stimulating intellectual circle. It included the brilliant philosopher Thomas Carlyle, and the critic and editor George Henry Lewes. Marian's wan complexion, large equine features, and serious demeanor contrasted with the depth and acuity of her mind and the brilliance of her conversation. Lewes had a broken complexion and was extremely short, but he was witty, urbane, and a versatile writer. When they met. Lewes' wife had recently deserted him and their three children; Marian Evans and he, defying **convention**, soon formed an attachment in which she accepted the role of wife, but without legal contract. The couple left immediately for a tour of Germany. Upon their return to London, many (but not all) of their free-thinking London friends accepted their action as a logical consequence of rationalistic beliefs. A great **irony** for many readers of Eliot's novels is the disparity between the consistent didacticism throughout her writing and the irregularity of her relationship with Lewes.

In 1857, at the urging of Lewes, she began to publish serially her first short stories and sketches under the pseudonym of George Eliot. (Notice Lewes' first name and the similarity between "Evans" and "Eliot.") The chronology of her work covers almost twenty years. *Scenes of Clerical Life* appeared in 1858. It is a work comprising three stories: "The Sad Fortunes of the Reverend Amos Barton," "Mr. Gilfil's Love Story," and "Janet's Repentance." Her first novel, *Adam Bede*, appeared in 1859 and was followed by *The Mill on the Floss* in 1860 and *Silas Marner* in 1861. These four titles form the body of her first period of work, based on the memories of her youth in Warwickshire. To many readers, her later novels fail to capture the imagination of these early ones, set in the rustic English countryside. Virginia Woolf, the twentieth-century novelist and critic, suggests that George Eliot is out of her element when she leaves the rustic scenes to portray higher levels of society. In *The Common Reader* Mrs. Woolf observes: "She is in the first place driven beyond the home world she knew and loved and forced to set foot in middle-class drawing rooms where young men sing all the summer morning and young women sit embroidering smoking-caps for bazaars. She feels herself out of her element, as her clumsy **satire** of what she calls 'good society' proves."

The middle period of her work includes *Romola*, a historical novel set in Florence, and *Felix Holt*, a political novel set in England during the era of the first Reform Bill. Her later period embraces *Middlemarch* (1871), a complex treatment of provincial life on its various levels. This novel, first published serially, is considered by many critics to be her masterpiece. Her final novel, *Daniel Deronda* (1876), presents a positive picture of Jewish life, perhaps the finest ever painted by a Christian author.

George Henry Lewes died in 1878. In November of the same year George Eliot published a book of essays called *The Impressions of Theophrastus Such*, probably written before

Lewes' death. George Eliot died two years later on December 22, 1880, a few months after marrying John W. Cross, who was her official biographer. Arranged by form, her major works include:

WORKS BY GEORGE ELIOT

Translations

1846 *Life of Jesus* by David Friedrich Strauss

1854 *Essence of Christianity* by Ludwig Andreas Feuerbach

Poems

1868 The Spanish Gypsy

1874 Jubal and Other Poems

Novels

1858 Scenes of Clerical Life

1859 Adam Bede

1860 The Mill on the Floss

1861 Silas Marner

1863 Romola

1866 Felix Holt the Radical

1871 Middlemarch

1876 Daniel Deronda

Essays

1879 Impressions of Theophrastus Such

CAREER

George Eliot, in the opinion of David Cecil, a modern critic of the Victorian novel, is the "first modern novelist." The first period of the English novel, he suggests, begins with Henry Fielding and ends with Anthony Trollope; the second, the period of Henry James, George Meredith, John Galsworthy and H. G. Wells, begins with George Eliot. Her art was intellectual; it was inspired by what she thought, and she used the novel to express her judgments on life. Her characters and scenes are secondary to her aim in fiction: the expression of a **theme**. She avoided the pat, happy endings of earlier novelists, if the logical working out of a character's situation demanded a tragic ending. Eliot, then, is a serious and moral novelist whose chief standard for judging people was based on the extent of their dedication to a life purpose. Her altruism is expressed in her writing goals: "My artistic purpose," she said, "is to present mixed human beings in such a way as to call forth tolerant judgment, pity and sympathy."

Her art ranges upon subjects taken from upper, middle, and the lower classes of small English towns or villages. The characterizations show careful research, indicative of the worth the author placed upon industry, restraint, and conscientiousness. Gradual development of character absorbs her-and is probably her most obvious forte. Basic changes which a character undergoes are carefully plotted and explained; we observe detailed, reflective explorations in the thinking of the characters of her novels. Usually a major character is confronted with a moral choice; he lives in a responsible world in which ethical values are strong; no acts are excused because a person is reduced merely to responding to an environment which determines what he will choose. The failure to live wisely is ultimately punished; secret remorse, if not public censure, functions as a nemesis for foolish or evil actions. Perhaps this poetic justice is at times unduly severe: to some the fate of John Raffles may appear capricious. To others, the somber tone of George Eliot's morality is supposedly relieved by the warm, simple humor of lower-class talk and gossip. Reserved for tavern and clerical characters and other "acceptable" types, it is quaint but hardly provoking.

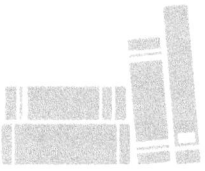

SILAS MARNER

TEXTUAL ANALYSIS

PART ONE: CHAPTER 1

....

In England during the early 1800s, men who earned a living by weaving cloth were usually looked upon with suspicion by the shepherds and peasants of the country villages. Even dogs barked at them as they went by, carrying their huge bags of raw materials. Anyone who had skill or knowledge of any kind was viewed with distrust-many villagers actually believed that weavers were under the influence of the Devil. Because people were unfriendly to them, most of the weavers lived alone and led lonely, odd lives.

Comment

We see that the novel opens several decades after machines began to replace individual English craftsmen. We also discover that in the remote villages, weavers were thought to possess some mysterious power or skill. Because no one was friendly to them, they were forced to live alone. The effect that loneliness has upon a man is one of the primary ideas that we will see developed in the early life of Silas Marner, the weaver of Raveloe.

Silas Marner lives near the small village of Raveloe in a stone cottage situated near a deep and dangerous hole where stone had formerly been excavated. He earns his living by weaving tablecloths, fancy napkins, and other linen goods for the women of Raveloe. In his house, he has a large wooden loom which makes a soft noise as he works. Sometimes, the young boys of Raveloe peep in his window to watch him. Silas does not like to waste time; to chase them he merely opens his door to stare at them with his large, piercing eyes. The boys run in fear because, like their parents, they are afraid of the simple weaver. Silas is often asked by the villagers to help cure people with rheumatism or other illnesses; they think he surely possesses some mysterious power.

Comment

The life that Silas Marner leads is a solitary one. He is rejected by all the people of Raveloe except when someone is ill. It is a curious fact, George Eliot observes, that at this time many country people in England did not believe in the power of God as much as they believed in the power of the Devil. People do not like Silas but they respect him because of the way he can sometimes cure sickness. Silas had no magical powers, for we learn later that he had acquired a knowledge of medicinal plants and herbs from his mother.

Situated in the middle region of England, Raveloe is far removed from the mainstream of life, it is at least an hour's ride on horseback to any of the main highways. Silas had come to this secluded spot fifteen years earlier from somewhere in Northern England. No one knew exactly where because Silas never spoke to anyone. He had always avoided the pretty girls of Raveloe and would never take time to visit the Rainbow tavern to chat with the men of the village but, once in a while, Silas became a topic for conversation. For example, once, Jem Rodney (the mole catcher) saw Silas, rigid and motionless, standing next to a fence. Jem thought Silas was dead because he didn't move at all-not even an eyelash. Jem shook him. Silas muttered "Good night" and went home. Some people thought he had a "fit" but Mr. Macey, clerk of the parish, believed that the strange conduct of the weaver was caused whenever Silas' soul left his body! Didn't Silas know a great deal about herbs? Didn't he cure Sally Oates when she was ill? Such a thing could happen to a man like Marner. It certainly could be said about him that he was odd and one further interesting fact: Silas Marner was a skillful weaver who had saved all his money for the past fifteen years. He must have a great deal of money hidden somewhere.

Comment

It is quite likely that the villagers in a small town like Raveloe might fail to understand why Silas Marner has strange seizures. Few people, at that time, knew very much about medicine so they did not realize that Silas suffered from catalepsy; a condition which causes a person's muscles to become rigid and his mind to go blank for a time. Silas never knew when he might get an attack nor could he remember anything that happened until after he regained consciousness. When he was much younger, Silas had two seizures of catalepsy, as we shall now see, which changed the entire course of his life.

Silas Marner was not always a lonely man. Years earlier, before he came to Raveloe, he was a young and happy man. He lived in a town in a section called Lantern Yard and was very active in a small church group in the community. One day, in church, Silas had one of his seizures at a prayer meeting. It lasted for over an hour and the members of the church, who knew Silas was a man of good example and faith, interpreted the incident as a sign of "special grace" from heaven for their fellow member. Silas' best friend was another weaver, William Dane. He was a very intelligent man who, unlike Silas, did not have a trusting, simple face. William Dane had narrow eyes and thin lips. He was always severely critical of his fellow church members or "brethren" because he said that he, at least, was positive that he was going to heaven when he died. He said the proof of this assurance of his own salvation came one day when he saw the words "calling and election (salvation) sure" mysteriously appear on the blank page of the Bible he had been reading shortly after he first joined the Lantern Yard Church Assembly. William Dane was also the only one who thought that Silas' seizure in church might have been caused by Satan (not God) entering into the soul of Silas. Silas, however, did not mind his friend's occasional rebukes, for he was in love. Silas was engaged to be married to a beautiful girl named Sarah who worked as a servant and who loved him very much. Silas used to visit her on Sundays and, sometimes, he would even ask William Dane to join them but, shortly after the incident in the church in which he had had the cataleptic attack, Silas noted that Sarah began to act differently towards him. Her manner changed so completely (from warmth to chilliness) that Silas finally asked her if she wished to break off their engagement. Afraid because she could offer the church members no good reason, Sarah refused to end their engagement; but something happened which soon made her change her mind.

Comment

The story of Silas is a story of change. We see now that he was not always a lonely, separated weaver. The seizure which took place in Church is interpreted as an evil sign by the person who is closest to Silas: William Dane. One can guess that the reason for the sudden change in attitude by Sarah may be because William Dane, whom we know is very critical of everyone except himself, may be influencing Sarah. In any event, we sense that something ominous is going to occur.

At this time, an elderly deacon of the church became dangerously ill and members of the community took turns caring for him day and night. Silas frequently took his turn at night; with William Dane relieving him at two o'clock in the morning. One night, when Silas was watching by the deacon's bedside, he noticed that the deacon's usually loud breathing had stopped. He was dead. Yet his death was very unusual, of the deacon had appeared to have regained much of his strength and everyone thought that he was on his way to recovery. Evidently the deacon had been dead for some time for his arms were rigid; it was now four o'clock in the morning. Silas wondered why William Dane had not come at two o'clock as he had expected. Silas awakened several friends, told them of the deacon's death, and then went home. At six o'clock, however, he was awakened. It was the minister of the church and William Dane. They asked Silas to come with them to the church, telling him coldly, "You shall hear." When they arrived at the prayer-meeting room, Silas found the rest of the church members waiting for them. Silas was seated in front of everyone as if he were the defendant in a trial. The minister showed him a pocket-knife and asked if it were his and where he had left it. Silas was frightened and said he did not know he had left it anywhere; the last time he remembered having it was when it was in his pocket. Then, the minister asked Silas not to hide his guilt but to confess and repent. The knife had been found in the bureau by the departed deacon's bedside. In addition, the bag of church money which was kept in the bureau was missing. The minister and the church members said the man who owned the knife was the man who stole the money. Silas was astonished. Finally, he said "God will clear me ... search my dwelling ... you will find nothing but my own savings, which William Dane knows I have had these six months." The minister, however, was not changed in his opinion of Silas' guilt: "No man was with our departed brother but you, for William Dane declares to us that he was hindered by sudden sickness from going to take his place as usual." Then, the minister also accused Silas of neglecting the dead body. Silas defended himself by saying that he must have slept or that he must have had another "visitation" or seizure. He thought the thief must have entered the room and stolen the money then. Once more, he urged them to search his dwelling. The search was made and ended by William Dane's finding the empty money bag behind a chest in Silas' room! William Dane asked his friend to confess. Silas replied simply, "God will clear me." Suddenly, Silas remembered where he last had his knife. "I remember now-the knife wasn't in my pocket," but he would say no more. William Dane said he didn't know what Silas meant. "God will clear me" is all that Silas would say. The members of the community decided to find out if Silas was guilty or innocent. They prayed and then drew lots to obtain a verdict. Choosing lots is similar to picking numbers from a hat but Silas confidently hoped that God would help him and that more "non-guilty votes" would be chosen than "guilty" ones. The lots declared that Silas Marner was guilty. Silas was immediately suspended from church membership and asked to surrender the stolen money. Only if he signed a confession to show that he had repented would he be admitted back into the church. Silas refused to admit to a crime he had not committed. Turning to William Dane, he said excitedly, "The last time I remember using my knife was when I took it out to cut a strap for you!" Silas accused William Dane of the crime and, in his great sorrow over what had happened to him, he cried out, "There is no God that governs the earth righteously, but a God of lies, that bears witness against the innocent!"

Then, Silas left and thought to himself about the girl he loved, Sarah: "Soon she will leave me, too." For an entire day, he sat alone. He was too upset even to go to Sarah to make her believe in his innocence. The second day, he began to work at his loom to escape from his thoughts; a few hours had passed when the minister and a deacon came with a message from Sarah. Their engagement, she felt, was broken. Silas said nothing; he turned to work at his loom. About a month later, Sarah was married to William Dane. Shortly thereafter, the brethren in Lantern Yard learned that Silas had left the town; never to return.

Comment

This part of the first chapter uses a flashback to give the reasons for Silas' failure to communicate with the people with whom he lives in Raveloe. Let us attempt to determine what probably happened the night the deacon died.

(1) Silas probably had a seizure just before William Dane came to relieve him at two o'clock. He would, therefore, be unaware of anything until he regained consciousness at four o'clock.

(2) William Dane may have suffocated the deacon for we know that he was recovering and probably did not die of natural causes.

(3) Dane probably removed the money from the drawer and then placed the knife that he had borrowed from Silas in the bureau.

(4) Dane then went to Silas' empty house, and "planted" the empty bag behind the chest in his room. He then went home and waited until the news of the deacon's death was brought to him.

(5) Arriving at the room where the deacon's death took place, Dane was the man who identified the knife as the one belonging to Silas. He then went (with the minister) to accuse Silas of the crime.

SUMMARY

The first chapter gives us the setting, in history, that we need to understand the reasons why much of the action occurs as it does. We discover that England at this time (the early nineteenth century) was primarily composed of small villages. Numerous trades still flourished before the industrial revolution, later in the century, forced many individual crafts out of business. The itinerant weaver in a community was believed to possess supernatural powers merely because he had acquired a certain skill in weaving cloth. The uneducated mind is never unwilling to imagine the impossible or to create fiction when no fact exists. So it is that Silas Marner becomes, like most outsiders in a narrow society, a social outcast. Yet, he is economically useful for he produces excellent linen goods at moderate prices; so he is, to a degree, accepted. Marner is industrious and thrifty: he flourishes and is, after fifteen years, known by all as a solitary but wealthy man.

We see that the villagers immediately mistake his catalepsy for a supernatural demon. However, they respect his knowledge of medicinal plants, a knowledge which sometimes enables him to cure illness when requested. However, the inhabitants of Raveloe know nothing of Marner's early life and disappointment. As a young man in Lantern Yard, he had been accused falsely by his friend, William Dane, of a crime he had not committed. It never occurred to the trusting Silas how foolish the church members were for choosing lots to find him guilty. Silas realized that he was merely the victim of a trap by William Dane, a trap that was based on the merest of circumstantial evidence. Yet, because he expected direct Divine intervention to prove his innocence, his simple faith was shattered when the luck of the lots went against him. He left Lantern Yard in deep despair; having lost all faith in man, woman, and God.

SILAS MARNER

TEXTUAL ANALYSIS

PART ONE: CHAPTER 2

The great change from Lantern Yard to Raveloe can only be imagined for Silas. All the familiar scenes and faces were gone and the God he trusted in (and was disappointed by) was not prayed to by men there as in the Lantern Yard Assembly. The first thing Silas did in Raveloe was to begin working at his loom. He received an order from Mrs. Osgood and worked far into the night to finish it earlier than she had expected.

Comment

Picture Silas at his loom working hour after hour like a spider weaving his web. Many people find physical activity a means of escaping from boredom. Imagine how anxious Silas must have been to forget his sorrowful experiences at Lantern Yard. Every hour at the loom helped him to forget the past.

When Silas brought Mrs. Osgood her finished linen, he was paid in gold guineas. Whenever he had been paid at Lantern Yard, he gave a portion of his wages to the Church. Now the money was all his; before, he needed money for a certain purpose. Now he began to love money for itself alone. Walking home from Mrs. Osgood's in the twilight, Silas took out the money from his pocket and "thought it was brighter in the gathering gloom."

Comment

Here is the first mention of the change in Silas towards money. He begins to lose his sense of values. Money itself becomes the chief purpose and satisfaction in his life. Because he has lost love for everything else in the "gloom" or darkness of his despair, he begins to fashion a love for hard, shiny metals: gold and silver.

Shortly after Silas arrived at Raveloe, an incident happened which made him become even more remote and separated from his neighbors in the village. One day, he gave the cobbler's ailing wife Sally Oates, some medicine he had made from foxglove (a small herb growing wild in the woods). Mrs. Oates found relief with the brown liquid mixture Silas had given her. When the other women of the village heard of the help that Sally Oates had received, they thought Silas had magical powers and they sought to have him prescribe medicines for them. Silas, however, knew he was no doctor and told all who came to him to keep their money; he would not cure them. No one believed him, though, when he said he knew no charms; everyone who had an accident or some misfortune thereafter traced its cause to Silas, saying that he probably had wished bad luck upon them.

Comment

It is not ironic that Silas' one attempt to show kindness to another human being results only in his further separation and loneliness?

So it was that year after year passed for Silas and the only friends he had were his gold and silver coins. Once, he broke a favorite earthenware vessel which he mended and retained as a memorial. His life was reduced to weaving at the loom and hoarding his money in an iron pot. For years, he worked sixteen hours a day and spent as little money as possible for food to keep up his strength. At night he joyfully counted his money. Silas was soon forced to keep all his gold and silver in two large, leather bags in a hole in the floor covered by bricks and sand. Each night, he would close his shutters, lock his door, brush away the sand and remove the bricks. He poured out the coins, spread them in heaps, and bathed his hands in them. He counted them and set them up in piles on the table; he felt their rounded outline with his thumb and fingers. Each coin was like a child to Silas; he would not have traded anyone of them for another. Silas had shrunk away from any thought other than his money; his heart was like a brook which had dried up into a thin, crooked crack in the earth. However, in that fifteenth year of Silas' life in Raveloe, something was about to happen during the Christmas season that was to blend his life with the lives of his neighbors.

Comment

Silas has become a miser. He loves the faces on his coins; not the faces of friends. He is like a prisoner in a cell who has nothing to do but to mark strokes on the wall to indicate the passage of time. Even wiser men than Silas may have devoted their lives to the unending pursuit of some goal because they have been cut off from faith and love.

SUMMARY

> The second chapter shows the reasons for the complete change in Silas; from the time he first comes to Raveloe (from Lantern Yard) until fifteen years later. He seeks consolation from his grief by working long hours at his loom. His attempt to help Sally Oates with the medicinal herbs has the ultimate result of making him even lonelier. Because of his despair, he transfers his love for people to a love for money. Silas himself is slowly transformed into a hoarding miser.

SILAS MARNER

TEXTUAL ANALYSIS

PART ONE: CHAPTER 3

In every small village there is usually one man who, because of his wealth and his family name, is more powerful than anyone else. The greatest man in Raveloe was Squire Cass. The title of Squire was given to him as a sign of respect because he was a country gentleman who owned a great deal of land. He did not work but received rent from farmers who lived on his land. England was at war with France so grain was expensive and his farmers were making great profits. Squire Cass knew they were prosperous and charged them higher rents than in peace-time. Every Christmas, many people would come to the Squire's home, the Red House. This was a large, handsome building almost directly across the street from the church. In those days, people would visit for days at a time at the holidays because travel conditions were poor and it was senseless to undergo an uncomfortable journey just for a brief visit. After the long feasting on beef and barrels of ale at the Squire's house, many people then visited Mrs. Osgood's, further up the village. The Squire's food was more abundant than

Mrs. Osgood's but hers was better prepared. This was because the Squires' wife had died and there was no woman living at the Red House to add the feminine touch.

Comment

This chapter introduces the second plot in the novel; the story of the Squire's son, Godfrey Cass. Later, we shall see how the action of this plot intersects with the action in the story of Silas Marner. Notice that the Squire's income is dependent upon the rent he collects from his tenant farmers; and that the custom of the prosperous land owner was to entertain for prolonged periods at the holidays throughout the year. Recall that the author indicated that something important was going to happen to Silas Marner during the Christmas season.

The Squire had several sons who did not work because he permitted them to be idle like himself. Godfrey Cass was the eldest. He was a friendly, good-natured and handsome young man who was first in line to inherit his father's land. His younger brother Dunstan or "Dunsey," as he was called, was a thick-set, heavy looking and mean kind of man who spent most of his time drinking or gambling. Most people in the village did not like Dunsey; nor did they particularly care what happened to him. They were concerned, however, that Godfrey, whom everyone liked, seemed to be going down the same road as Dunsey. Godfrey had been away from home for days at a time. It looked, for a while, as if he were going to marry the pretty Nancy Lammeter. She was Mrs. Osgood's niece (Nancy's mother had died) who came to live at the Red House. However, she had heard about Godfrey's recent conduct and, if Godfrey failed to turn over a new leaf, he might lose her.

Comment

Our first reaction is to favor Godfrey over Dunsey. Our decision in based on the quality of the person's character and, here, the difference between the two brothers is obvious. We also learn of the romantic bond which exists between Nancy Lammeter and Godfrey. Our curiosity is provoked when we learn that Godfrey has often been absent from the Red House for long periods of time. In the next scene, we discover why.

It is late November in that fifteenth year of Silas Marner's life at Raveloe. The setting is a parlour of the Red House. It is late afternoon and the fading light is shining on Godfrey Cass who stands before the fire with an angry look on his face. The door opens; it is Dunsey. His face is flushed from excessive drinking. Angrily, Godfrey tells him that he must hand over the one hundred pounds rent from Fowler (a farmer) to the Squire; or else admit that he gave it to Dunsey. The Squire, it seems, is threatening to seize Fowler's goods if the rent is not paid within a week. Dunsey refuses flatly to pay back the rent money he has borrowed from Godfrey saying, "You'll not refuse me the kindness to pay it back for me. I might tell the Squire how his handsome son was married to that nice young woman, Molly Farren, and was very unhappy because he couldn't live with his drunken wife." Godfrey seizes Dunsey by the arm and excitedly insists, "I have no money: I can get no money." Godfrey had borrowed money from a man named Kimble but he would not lend Godfrey any more. Dunstan suggests that Godfrey sell his beautiful horse, Wildfire, at the hunt the next morning but Godfrey is planning to go to a party at Mrs. Osgood's house the next night and does not wish to return home late and dirty from the hunt. Dunsey begins to tease Godfrey about the party and Nancy Lammeter; "And there's sweet Miss Nancy coming; and we shall dance with her, and promise never to be naughty again, and be taken into favor, and - " Godfrey turns red with anger. Dunsey sits in a chair and begins to tap the end of his whip in the palm of his hand. He reminds Godfrey that his secret wife, Molly Farren, is also a drug addict. Next he hints at an evil solution to Godfrey's problem (about being unable to marry Nancy since he already has a wife) by wondering what might happen "... if Molly should happen to take a drop of laudanum (a liquid made from opium) someday, and make a widower of you. Nancy wouldn't mind being a second, if she didn't know it." Godfrey becomes pale. He wonders if he should tell the Squire everything. He knows that Molly Farren may tell of their marriage because he has not enough money for her. "You drain me of money till I have got nothing to pacify her with, and she'll do as she threatens someday. It's all one. I'll tell my father everything myself, and you may go to the devil." Finally, Godfrey agrees to let Dunsey ride his horse to the hunt the next morning to sell him. However, he warns him to be careful not to drink for he might seriously injure himself or Wildfire. Dunsey laughs confidently and then leaves.

Comment

This is one of the most important scenes in the novel, so far, because it presents the background on the chief problems that Godfrey Cass must attempt to solve. Dunsey Cass is black-mailing his brother. He knows that Godfrey entered into a degrading marriage with Molly Farren; a woman whose weaknesses were both alcoholic and narcotic. It was an ugly story of low passion that the author does not fully explain except to tell us that the marriage was a trap laid by Dunstan's cunning so that he could satisfy his jealous hate of Godfrey and obtain blackmail money from him. Godfrey has several things to worry about:

(1) He has given the rent money from Fowler to Dunstan and now must sell his horse, Wildfire, to get enough cash to pay the Squire.

(2) The Squire may find out about his marriage and turn him out of the house in disgrace.

(3) If Nancy Lammeter learns his secret she will refuse to see him. Although he cannot ask her to marry him because of his marriage, he does love her and enjoys her companionship above anything else.

After Dunsey left, Godfrey was alone with his thoughts. He thought of the four years he had courted Nancy; of how he could have changed his idle habits and become a good husband to her. Now, however, that was impossible, and his situation would be worse if his ugly secret was discovered. Both his father and Nancy would turn their backs on him then. He would lose both his inheritance and the one woman who could have changed his life for the better. Godfrey, wishing to escape his bitter thoughts, decides to spend another idle evening at the Rainbow tavern.

Comment

We have seen how Silas Marner changed; now we see that another good-humored, affectionate person can become hate-filled towards life when he thinks of the sorrow his own wrong-doing has caused. Silas was the victim of chance and the evil of others; Godfrey was guilty of willfully committing an act but he was, also, the victim of his brother's disgraceful plotting.

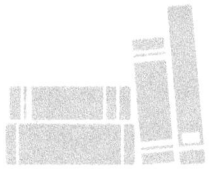

SILAS MARNER

TEXTUAL ANALYSIS

PART ONE: CHAPTER 4

The next morning, Dunstan Cass sets out to sell Wildfire at the hunt. It is a wet, foggy day and, when he passes the cottage of Silas Marner, he notices that the deserted stone pit is filled to the brim with red, muddy water. He hears Silas' loom through the mist and suddenly thinks of frightening the old weaver into giving him money to pay the debts he owes. Then, he decides that he will receive enough money from the sale of Wildfire to satisfy Godfrey so he continues on his way. At Batherley, he sells the horse to a man named Bryce for one hundred and twenty pounds; the money to be paid only after Wildfire is delivered safe and sound to the Bryce stables. However, Dunsey, foolishly drinking and swaggering, then decides to ride Wildfire in the hunt. Unfortunately, the horse is soon killed, pierced by a sharp stake when it fails to clear a fence in a jump. Dunsey had exhausted its energy by forcing it to jump excessively. Now that Wildfire is dead, there will be no money to give to Godfrey. Dunstan is uninjured; he swears, takes another drink, and begins walking back to Raveloe … swishing the riding whip he had taken from Godfrey that morning. The name Godfrey Cass was cut in deep letters on the golden handle. (This is an important fact to remember for the whip is discovered much later in the story.) The road is covered with fog and the falling rain makes the ground slippery. Suddenly, seeing a light coming from Silas Marner's cottage, Dunstan thinks of borrowing money from him. After receiving no answer to his knock, Dunstan is surprised to find that the door is unlocked and the cottage empty. Silas has gone on a short errand. A piece of meat tied with string and fastened at the other end to Silas' huge door key is dangling near the fire roasting slowly. Silas never bought very much meat because it was expensive, and he did not buy the proper utensils with which to cook it in his fireplace. This piece of pork was a gift from Priscilla Lammeter, Nancy's sister. Because he used to hang his door key on a pot hanger suspended above the fire, he could not lock his door when he left to go to the village to purchase some twine for his loom. Dunstan knows that Marner probably keeps his money in his cottage. Why not steal the money? Searching the room, Dunstan Cass brushes away the sand, removes the bricks in the floor, and lifts out the two heavy bags of gold hidden in the hole. He then replaces the bricks and sand, and leaves, closing the door behind him carefully. Dunsey, holding the whip and the heavy gold, begins to step away through the darkness and the mist.

Comment

The theft of the weaver's gold is an action which joins the plot of *Silas Marner* with the plot of Godfrey Cass. Notice how the author skillfully plans the circumstances leading up to the reasons why Dunstan would be at the cottage of Silas and why Silas would be absent. Silas did not want to waste time, the following morning, away from his loom, so he went to Raveloe that night for twenty minutes while his food was being cooked. Even the reason for the door's being open when Dunstan arrived is logically explained by the use which Silas made of the door key.

SILAS MARNER

TEXTUAL ANALYSIS

PART ONE: CHAPTER 5

....

Silas returns home just a few minutes after Dunstan Cass has left. He never dreamed that any thief would steal from him, and, for fifteen years, no one had even attempted to do so. Entering his cottage, he scuffs over the footprints Dunstan had left in the sand, puts down his lantern, and the sack with the twine, and resumes his preparation for dinner. Wishing to count his gold while eating his dinner, Silas sweeps away the sand without perceiving any change and removes the bricks. Gone! His hand trembles. Again and again, he looks; he searches the entire house ... in vain. Finally, he sits down at his loom and begins to wonder: Was it a thief or some "unseen power" that stole his money? Silas thinks and thinks; at last, he decides that the man who robbed him must be Jem Rodney.

Comment

Silas believes Jem is the thief for three reasons:

(1) Jem was known to be a poacher; that is, he trespassed illegally on other people's land to hunt game.

(2) Once Jem had made a jesting remark to Silas about his money.

(3) Jem had come in to light his pipe at Silas' fire one night and lingered there instead of leaving immediately.

To catch the thief, Silas knows he needs help from the people of the village. He runs out into the rain to the Rainbow tavern where he knows the men of the town often gathered in the evening.

SILAS MARNER

TEXTUAL ANALYSIS

PART ONE: CHAPTER 6

This chapter is viewed by some as one of the finest chapters in English literature because of the outstanding picture of small village characters (and their conversation) which George Eliot has drawn for us. The scene is in the kitchen of the Rainbow tavern where the less prosperous men of the village sit, smoke, and talk. The butcher is questioned about a Durham cow he says he has purchased from Mr. Lammeter. However, the farrier (cow veterinary) tells the butcher that he knows that the cow was drenched (given medicine for sickness). The landlord of the Rainbow, Mr. Snell, is the peacemaker when disputes arise; he changes the subject. Mr. Macey, the elderly clerk, and Ben Winthdrop, the wheel maker, tease Mr. Tookey, the worried little deputy-clerk, about his poor singing voice and his ambition to better himself. Again, the landlord changes the subject by asking Mr. Macey about his brother Solomon, who plays the fiddle. This question soon prompts Mr. Macey to tell a long narrative about how the first Mr. Lammeter came to Raveloe years before and about the marriage of his son, the present Mr. Lammeter. The others in the Rainbow have heard Mr. Macey's stories many times but they love to hear them again. Mr. Macey then retells the history of the Warrens, the Lammeter estate, and of Mr. Cliff, the mad tailor from "Lunnon" (London) who used to own it.

The Lammeter stables are still called "Cliff's Holiday" and are, supposedly, inhabited by ghosts. Mr. Dowlas, the cow doctor, scoffing at such an idea, is willing to wager that no ghosts are in the stables. However, the landlord and, especially, Mr. Macey believe in ghosts and consider someone who does not to be ignorant.

Comment

Notice that no action in the novel occurs in this chapter. Rather, we have a warm, humorous scene described with realistic dialogue and marked insight into character. Contrast this chapter with the previous one's gloomy and depressing tone.

The fact that the men are discussing ghosts is deliberately planned to make the entrance of Silas more effective dramatically.

SILAS MARNER

TEXTUAL ANALYSIS

PART ONE: CHAPTER 7

Just then, Silas Marner enters the room silently. He is dripping wet and staring with his large, strange eyes. The men are startled and jerk their long pipes like insects waving their antennae. Silas does have an unearthly, ghostly appearance. The landlord is the first to speak to Silas: "What's your business?" Silas can utter only: "Robbed! I've been robbed." He demands that he be taken to the constable or to Squire Cass or Mr. Crackenthorp. The Landlord thinks Silas is mad and tells Jem Rodney, who is closest to the weaver, to seize him. Jem, however, refuses and seizes his drinking can when Silas asks him if he stole the money. Silas is forced to sit and tell his story from the beginning.

Comment

The unusual situation in which Silas finds himself is that he is now mixing among his fellow men. He needs their help and they are interested in his problem. This scene marks the beginning of the stirring of feeling inside Silas for his neighbors ... for the first time in fifteen years.

Most of the men who listen sympathetically to the account of the robbery believe that the devil is probably the one who has stolen the money. They have difficulty, however, trying to estimate why the devil waited until the door was unlocked before attempting to take it. The landlord defends Jem Rodney and is supported by Mr. Macey. They tell Silas that Jem has been with them in the tavern. Silas approaches Jem says, "I was wrong," admitting that Jem was the first person he had thought of as the robber; because he had been in Silas' home more than anyone else.

Comment

Jem Rodney is freed of suspicion of the robbery. Once more, Silas is forced to come to think about others; in his sorrow for accusing Jed, he shows pity for him, also.

Silas tells the farrier he has lost two hundred and seventy-two pounds of money (which, by today's standards, would be the equivalent of a fortune). The farrier suggests that Silas go with two of the "sensibilest" men of the group to the constable, Master Kench. The farrier knows the constable is ill and he is hoping to be appointed deputy. However, Mr. Macey intervenes and says that the law "forbids" cow doctors to be deputies. The farrier objects and disagrees with a law which would prevent him from receiving the honor of deputy. The landlord, as usual, makes peace and Mr. Dowlas (the farrier) and another man leave with Silas who must once again go out into the rain.

> **Comment**

It is significant to observe that the townspeople themselves, as well as Silas, are beginning to soften their hearts.

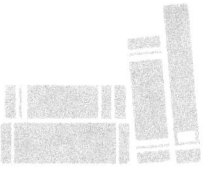

SILAS MARNER

TEXTUAL ANALYSIS

PART ONE: CHAPTER 8

The next morning, the entire village is excited with the news of the robbery. The rain has washed away all footprints at the stone pits but a tinder-box (a small box which holds kindle and which is ignited by sparks from striking flint rock with steel) is found, in the mud, in the vicinity. It is not Silas' box, although some suspicious people think it is. Mr. Macey does not believe the tinder box is a clue because he still argues that spirits have made off with the money. Mr. Crackenthorp (the rector of the church), Squire Cass, and other men of importance think that the tinder-box may belong to a dark-skinned peddler, who had recently been in Raveloe selling his trinkets and wares. Mr. Crackenthorp is curious: "Did he wear earrings?" Mr. Snell gives an evasive answer, trying to say "yes" and "no" at the same time. Others are questioned and, eventually, it is decided that the peddler did wear earrings.

Comment

Here George Eliot gives us further insight into the life of a small community of this period. We perceive that the robbery has the effect of making the comparatively dull members of the community suddenly become excitable. Observe how each is ready to believe the wildest interpretation without having the facts necessary for proof. The passage about the earrings is especially humorous because the truth of whether the peddler wore them or not makes no difference in his guilt or innocence.

Silas is questioned about the peddler but he says that he did not permit him to enter his house. Silas is hoping that the peddler might be the culprit and he can readily picture his gold in the peddler's box. The people in the village think the peddler is guilty and are not ready to believe Silas because:

(1) Silas has poor eyesight from the close work he has done at his loom over the years. He would not see a man prowling near his house as other men would.

(2) Some people believe that Silas is a half-crazy miser and that his testimony about the peddler cannot be believed.

(3) Men who wear rings are known to be criminals sometimes. The villagers assume erroneously, therefore, that the peddler (whom they think wears earrings) is the thief.

Godfrey Cass, meanwhile, had returned from Mrs. Osgood's party and had gone to bed without worrying about Dunstan because he realized that, perhaps, Dunstan had to wait a day to sell Wildfire. Another possibility was that he may have slept in Batherley at the Red Lion Inn instead of coming home in the fog. Down at the Rainbow, the next day, he meets Mr. Snell and tells him he thought the peddler a "merry, grinning fellow" and it is all nonsense about his evil looks. Some think Godfrey will go to the town of Tarley to find the peddler to prove Mr. Snell is wrong. Godfrey, however, mounts his horse and heads, not toward Tarley, but toward Batherley. Hoping to find Dunstan and annoyed with himself for trusting his horse to him, he rides until he finally meets Bryce, who tells him that the body of Wildfire has been found. Godfrey conceals his great fear and leaves. On the way back to Raveloe, Godfrey debates about telling his father that he gave the Fowler's rent money to Dunstan. He knows he has done wrong by giving the money to his worthless brother but he does not wish his father to think he spent it on himself: "I'd never have spent the money for my own pleasure," he muses, "I was tortured into it." Godfrey thinks his father may not be so severe with him if he explains how Dunstan blackmailed him for the money. He may also tell his father about his secret marriage; perhaps, the Squire would prefer to keep the marriage a secret to protect his own pride. Godfrey knew his father has a careless habit of permitting situations to worsen and suddenly taking severe measures to correct them. For example, the Squire often permitted his tenant farmers to neglect their fences, fail to pay their rent, and, in general, to manage their farms poorly; but, when he needed money, he was extremely demanding with them and would not listen to any appeal. With these thoughts, Godfrey goes to bed, promising himself to tell the Squire everything the next morning. However, when he awakes, all he can think of are the consequences:

(1) His disgrace with his father.

(2) His complete and final loss of Nancy Lammeter.

Godfrey changes his mind again. He will not tell his father; perhaps, Dunstan will return in a few days with money and all will be well.

Comment

In this chapter, we witness the hopelessness of the villagers in attempting to solve the theft of Marner's gold: much of their debating and theorizing is amusing, especially that part of it which attempts to fix the blame upon the peddler. We see how irrelevant their approach is to the evidence. For example, when they spend time determining if the peddler wore earrings or not, they are merely quarreling among themselves. The second string of the plot in this chapter belongs to Godfrey. We see his disappointment upon discovering that Wildfire has been killed, and we wonder if he is going to tell all to his father. However, as the chapter ends, we find that Godfrey's chief weaknesses (indecision and timidity) are still with him. He lives on in his world of appearance; both his father and Nancy are deceived but, to tell them the truth, means to shatter his own happiness. This act Godfrey is unable to do.

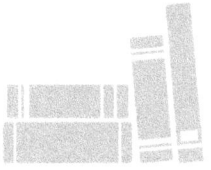

SILAS MARNER

TEXTUAL ANALYSIS

PART ONE: CHAPTER 9

The chapter begins with a description of Squire Cass, before breakfast, on the morning that Godfrey is to speak with him about the rent money which he gave to Dunstan. About sixty years of age, Godfrey's father is tall and stout. He has a knitted brow but a "slack, feeble mouth." He is careless in his personal habits; his dress is slovenly. Yet, he has no superior in the village; so, he speaks with great authority. He views everything he owns as the oldest and the best. Godfrey approaches him at the table and tells him first, that Wildfire was injured; finally, he admits that Dunsey has killed the horse. He also reveals that he has lent Fowler's rent to his brother. The Squire becomes purple with anger. He reminds Godfrey that he is not required, by law, to leave his money or lands to Godfrey when he dies. He wishes to speak with Dunsey, fearing some kind of trick is being attempted, "and you've been bribing him not to tell."

Comment

Imagine how frightened Godfrey is when his father suggests that there may be something hidden which Godfrey does not reveal. The dramatic value in the scene resides in the reader's knowledge; knowledge that a character (the Squire) does not possess.

The Squire is determined to disown Dunstan, "to turn him out without a cent." He tells Godfrey that he is disappointed with his conduct, especially in light of the possible marriage he had anticipated between Godfrey and Nancy Lammeter. He asks Godfrey if, perhaps, she had refused his marriage proposal. Godfrey admits that she hasn't but he does not think she will accept. The Squire laughs at this comment, expressing an opinion that Nancy's father would not be unwilling to have his daughter marry into the family. He tells Godfrey to ask her to marry him now; if Godfrey refuses, he shall disown him. He ends by telling Godfrey to sell Dunsey's horse for the money because he will not permit him to live at the Red House any longer. The Squire says, "He shan't hang him on me anymore."

Comment

Godfrey has both freed himself and made his chains stronger. On the one hand, he has told his father two important truths:

(1) He has given the one hundred pounds' rent money to Dunstan.

(2) Dunstan has killed Wildfire, Godfrey's valuable horse.

In both instances, Godfrey has fared much better than he had expected. His father scolds him for being foolish enough to lend both the rent and, later, the horse to Dunsey. He decides to turn Dunsey out of the house, forever; yet, on the other hand, Godfrey has made his trouble worse:

(1) His father demands that he ask Nancy to marry him or he will disown him, too.

(2) He cannot marry Nancy, even if she consents, because of his secret marriage to Molly Farren. He would be forced to refuse her if she did wish to marry him.

Godfrey is unrealistic. The chapter ends with his choosing to leave things alone; in the hope that chance will resolve his difficulties. Similarly, the author adds, many men spend more than they earn, neglect their responsibilities, betray friendships and secrets, and attempt ambitions beyond their power in the belief that chance will create success. The one thing such people pray against is the one thing they can be certain of: that a certain seed bears a certain fruit. In other words, chance cannot change that which is certain to happen.

SILAS MARNER

TEXTUAL ANALYSIS

PART ONE: CHAPTER 10

Justice Malan of Tarley, a magistrate, supervises the investigation of the robbery of Silas Marner's money. The chief suspect is the peddler and a lengthy description of him: "curly black hair," "wearing large rings," and so forth is spread throughout the countryside. Many peddlers, however, fit this description so it is impossible to trace the blame to a single one. Weeks pass and people soon lose interest in the case. Excitement has died down in Raveloe, also. No one even misses Dunstan Cass who has not been seen since the day he killed Wildfire, Godfrey's horse. Once before, Dunstan had been gone from home for a long period of time. The villagers of Raveloe do not suspect Dunstan of the robbery even though he disappeared on the same day that Marner's money was stolen.

Comment

It is logical that Dunstan is not suspected as the thief:

(1) The Cass family, with its proud ancestry and wealth, would not ordinarily be associated with any crime whatsoever. People in Raveloe hesitate to suggest evil of reputable families.

(2) Christmas time is coming and the gaiety of the season, with its abundance of puddings and drink, dulls the minds of many people.

Down at the Rainbow tavern, the opinion of the robbery is divided into two viewpoints:

(1) Some feel that there is a logical explanation for the loss of the money. They maintain that the clue of the tinder box fixes the blame upon the peddler.

(2) Others suggest that the only way to view the robbery is as a supernatural mystery which can never be solved.

Silas Marner himself feels a profound sense of loss because his money has been stolen. To other people, his life has been withered and shrunken (as it was) but, to Silas, it has been an eager life. The money has been the one thing he could cling to; it is the only thing that has satisfied him. Now, it is gone. Silas still has his loom and his work, of course, but the prospect of counting his money each night is over. He can receive no delight from the new money he makes for it only reminds him of how much he has lost. He fills up his unhappy life by weaving; at night, now that he cannot count his money, he sits by his fire, leans his elbows on his knees, clasps his head with his hands, and moans softly.

Comment

The love that Silas had for people was lost years ago at Lantern Yard when he was accused falsely of stealing money. At Raveloe, he had created a new love; for money. The stealing of his gold, however, leaves him with nothing to love. Notice how Eliot has paralleled the early life of Silas with his current experience. In both instances, a robbery was instrumental in causing Silas' great sorrow.

The villagers in Raveloe begin to show affection and charity towards Silas. Mrs. Osgood sends him various gifts of food; as do other people who have made extra puddings and roasts for the Christmas season. Mr. Crackenthorp, the rector at the church, gives Silas some pigs' feet. Many people stop in at Silas' cottage to ask him to repeat the details of the robbery; or to try to cheer him.

Mr. Macey, the village clerk, visits Silas and gives him a long talk; advising him not to sit moaning about his money. He asks Silas if he has a Sunday suit because he is anxious to have Silas attend weekly services at Church. Silas replies that he does not own such a suit. Mr. Macey promises then to have his assistant, Mr. Tookey, make a suit at a low price so that Silas may come to Church and "be a bit neighborly." Silas is unsure, though, about going to church for he has not gone in fifteen years. Mr. Macey leaves, thinking Silas is so "muddled" that he probably does not even know when Sunday comes around each week.

Another person who comes to comfort Silas is Mrs. Dolly Winthrop, wife of the wheel maker, Ben Winthrop. She is a kind, patient woman who seeks out the sadder and more serious things in life so that she can be of help. She always seems to find time to visit someone who is ill or needs her assistance. The good, wholesome woman is aware of the suffering of Silas and, one Sunday afternoon, she visits him; taking her little seven-year-old boy, Aaron, with her. Dolly has baked lard cakes for Silas but she cannot read the lettering on them. Aaron is shy and hides behind one of Silas' chairs. Silas reads the lettering; it is "I.H.S." (initials representing the name of Christ.) He then thanks Dolly for bringing the cakes. Dolly wishes to have Silas begin to attend church and she speaks to him; trying to persuade him. Silas tells her that he has never been to a Raveloe church but that he had belonged to a small chapel (Lantern Yard) years ago. Again Dolly, recommends that Silas go to church. Aaron asks for another cake and, soon, Dolly makes him sing for Silas. Aaron sings "God rest you, merry gentlemen." Silas thanks him but he has not been listening carefully at all. Mrs. Winthrop and Aaron leave after she makes one final attempt to win Silas to churchgoing.

Notwithstanding the attempts of Mr. Macey and Dolly Winthrop, Silas spends his Christmas day alone. No one could ever suspect that he was once a man who loved others with tenderness.

Every Christmas, Doctor Kimble (who loved to recall his early experiences as a doctor) and his wife came to the home of Squire Cass to drink spirits and to play cards. The great celebration at the Red House, however, was not on Christmas but on New Year's Eve. Every year, the Squire held a dance and all the society of Raveloe and Tarley came and stayed for several days. Godfrey was looking forward to the long, happy days of the New Year's Eve celebration but, in his mind, he could hear the voice of Anxiety whispering to him that Dunsey might come home; that more money might be needed (Godfrey would have to sell his dead mother's diamond pin) and that Squire Cass might attempt to bring Nancy and Godfrey into a marriage match which Godfrey could only decline. Then, Godfrey thought only of looking into Nancy's eyes. He joined the noisy Christmas company and did much drinking; yet, even then, he could still hear the voice of Anxiety.

SUMMARY

In this chapter we discover:

(1) The people soon forget about the robbery of Silas' gold; they assume that the peddler is guilty.

(2) No one suspects Dunstan Cass of the robbery.

(3) Silas is deep in sorrow and gloom after his loss; although the townspeople begin to show greater fondness and charity towards him, he seems unable to respond. Both Mr. Macey and Dolly Winthrop are unsuccessful in their attempts to interest Silas in church.

(4) Godfrey's situation has not changed. He looks forward to the New Year's Eve dance for the happiness it will bring. He pushes out of his mind, as best he can, thoughts of his problems or of the future.

SILAS MARNER

TEXTUAL ANALYSIS

PART ONE: CHAPTER 11

Nancy Lammeter arrives at the Red House for the long festivities of New Year's; she rides (sitting side-saddle) on a little pillow ... on the same horse as her Father. Godfrey helps her down and she enters the house to be greeted by Mrs. Kimble (the doctor's wife and the sister of Squire Cass). She goes upstairs to the Blue Room where her clothes boxes had been sent; here, the other ladies are grooming themselves for a before-dinner tea. In the room, Nancy sees six young ladies; including a pair of unattractive sisters from the city of Lytherly. The two Miss Gunns are dressed in the height of fashion; perhaps even beyond good taste. Nancy talks to Mrs. Osgood (her aunt) exchanging pleasant greetings. Mrs. Osgood likes Nancy very much and has given her some family jewelry as presents even though Nancy has refused to marry Gilbert Osgood because he is a cousin. (Nancy's dead mother and Mrs. Osgood were sisters.) Three of the ladies leave the room but he Gunn sisters remain; curious to see what kind of gown a country girl like Nancy might have. Nancy unpacks her boxes; revealing her beautiful, costly, and well-kept clothes.

The Gunn sisters notice privately that Nancy is truly a lady in her dress and manners. Only her hands are not as pretty as they might otherwise be because she performs many chores at home. Also, Nancy mispronounces certain words saying, for example, "mate" for "meat" and "oss" for "horse".

Nancy's sister, Priscilla Lammeter, bursts into the room. She is five years older than Nancy and lacks the beauty and grace of her younger sister. Priscilla is a frank, talkative, tactless person who will say what she thinks; regardless of what others may think. She knows she has a ruddy complexion, and is not, perhaps, very attractive to men but she does not care about men anyway. She prefers to remain single and to be independent; saying, "Mr. Have-Your-Own-Way is the best husband." Priscilla wears the same color dress that Nancy wears because Nancy wishes them to look like sisters. Priscilla knows she will not appear as pretty even when the dress is just as pretty. "For I am ugly," she says; then, turning to the Gunn sisters, she adds, "But, law! I don't mind, do you?"

Nancy and Priscilla descend the stairs and enter the parlour. Mr. Crackenthorp, the rector, makes a playful remark to Nancy about Godfrey after Godfrey leads her to a seat next to him. Squire Cass is in a jovial mood and speaks to the rector and Mrs. Crackenthorp (a small, mousy type of woman) about Nancy's great beauty. Mr. Lammeter hears the compliment but does not let it appear that he is gratified or elated at the possibilities of a marriage between his daughter and Godfrey; not unless there is an alteration in Godfrey's conduct will he give his consent.

Doctor Kimble, his wife, the Squire, and Priscilla Lammeter have a conversation about Priscilla's cooking and Mrs. Kimble's. Dr. Kimble complains laughingly that his wife puts black pepper in his food whenever he offends her. He calls it "an awful tit-for-tat."

Comment

We are shown realistic scenes like this one throughout the book. Recall the pleasant recording of country conversation heard in the scene at the Rainbow Tavern. It is characteristic of the skill of George Eliot that she can capture the mood of gaiety in a few lines, transmitting it to the reader in authentic, idiomatic nineteenth century speech.

Solomon Macey is an old, white-haired man whom the Squire asks to play the fiddle for the company. The chairs are pushed back and everyone follows him into the White Parlour (where the mistletoe and holly are hung) to begin the dance. The Squire leads the dance with Mrs. Crackenthorp; joining hands with the Rector and Mrs. Osgood. Mr. Macey watches them as they dance. He observes that the Squire is rather spry "considering his weight" and that the rector "might do worse, he might do worse." Ben Winthrop, the husband of Dolly, is there with Aaron; watching and also making comments. Aaron wishes to know if one of the feathers in a woman's hat is actually sticking out of her head! Nancy and Godfrey are dancing; Ben remarks that Nancy is a lovely girl. Mr. Macey is critical of Godfrey for permitting himself to be influenced by Dunsey and for letting him have Wildfire, for this resulted in the death of the horse. Both he and Ben wonder if the young couple will eventually be united in marriage.

Nancy and Godfrey suddenly leave the dance floor because Squire Cass has stepped on the train of Nancy's dress. Priscilla hurries to fetch thread and needle as Godfrey and Nancy wait in a small parlour adjoining the dance. Nancy is sorry for causing trouble but Godfrey tells her that one dance with her means more to him than any other pleasure in the world. Nancy disagrees because of Godfrey's past action towards her. She admits she would like to see a change in him but she refuses to encourage him. Godfrey accuses her of having no feeling for him but she replies. "I think those have the least feeling that act wrong to begin with." A quarrel is about to ensue but Priscilla enters. Boldly, Godfrey asks Nancy if she wants him to leave. Nancy leaves the decision to him. Godfrey, determined to get as much joy as possible out of each moment because he fears the future, answers, "Then I like to stay."

SUMMARY

> The chapter opens with Nancy's arrival at the Red House for the beginning of the New Year's festivities. We notice:
>
> (1) The expected custom, in rural England at the holiday season, was to have lavish expenditures of food and drink presented by the chief men of prominence and wealth in the community.
>
> (2) Nancy Lammeter is a refined woman of taste and manner although she has not received a full education.
>
> (3) Priscilla Lammeter is a foil, or mirror, for her sister. She represents the unsophisticated, realistic kind of woman one might expect to find in a community far removed from cultural advantages; yet, we like her much more than the Gunn sisters who, for all their knowledge of fashion and education, lack the basic human warmth of Priscilla and her sister.
>
> (4) The social aspects of English life in this period are captured in the description and conversation of numerous secondary characters such as Dr. Kimble, his wife, Ben

Winthrop, the Rector, Mr. Macey, and his brother, Solomon Macey, the fiddler.

(5) Nancy is decidedly interested in Godfrey, but Godfrey's situation remains unchanged. He loves her but he cannot marry her because he is secretly married to Molly Farren; a woman addicted to alcohol and drugs.

SILAS MARNER

TEXTUAL ANALYSIS

PART ONE: CHAPTER 12

While Godfrey was speaking to Nancy Lammeter, his wife (Molly Farren) was walking in the snow to Raveloe carrying her child in her arms. She was dressed in rags and shivered with each step. Her purpose was to go to the Red House to reveal that she was Godfrey's wife. She wished to disgrace him for he had said that he would sooner die than admit that she was his wife. Godfrey had given her enough money on which to live but she had always spent it on opium (at this time there were no laws against its scale). Molly had set out at an early hour but had lingered; hoping the snow would stop. Now, it was seven o'clock and the snow was deep. She had a bottle of Laudanum (liquid opium) and took a drink. Emptying it, she threw the bottle away. Soon, however, she became drowsy and wanted to sleep. Still clutching the child tightly in her arms, she lay down on a small furze bush in the snow to sleep. The drink had numbed her senses; she could not feel the cold of the snow nor the freezing wind. Soon, her fingers lost their tension and the child cried, "Mammy," but the mother's ear was deaf to any sound.

The child rolled from the mother and began walking in the snow towards a bright light from a cottage. The light came from the fire of Silas Marner's cottage. Slowly, the child made its way through the snow until it reached the door and the door was wide open! Walking directly to the warm fireplace, the child sat down before the fire; happy and contented. Soon she fell asleep.

And where was Silas Marner when this small visitor arrived? He was in the cottage but he did not see the child. Since the robbery, Marner had developed the habit of opening his door several times each night and looking out to see if someone might be coming to his house with the lost gold. Some of the villagers had told him that he should sit up on New Year's Eve to welcome the new year because it might bring him good luck. Several times, he had opened the door and had looked to see if anyone were coming. Once a dark figure (Molly Farren) could actually be seen walking through the snow, but Silas did not see her for he had suddenly been seized with a cataleptic attack. He stood there, rigid and motionless, with his right hand on the open door and did not see the child enter his home.

Comment

We see why the door is open when the child approaches the cottage. Silas is still susceptible to the seizures and one occurs when he has opened the door hoping to see someone returning with his gold.

When his senses finally return, Silas turns to fix the logs in his fire; suddenly, he thinks he sees his gold before the hearth! He reaches out to touch it but he feels warm curls rather than the hard outline of his coins. Amazed, Silas kneels; bending his head to examine the beautiful little girl. At first, he thinks the child may be his little sister, Hephzibah, who died when he was a small boy. Or is it a dream? Silas has not realized that the child entered when he had the seizure at the open door. Silas picks up the child, feeds her porridge with brown sugar, and removes her wet boots. He realizes that she must have been walking in the snow in order to have wet her feet. Picking up the child, he opens his door and follows the small footprints which she had made in the snow. The child soon cries, "Mammy," and Silas is then aware that in the bush before him is a snow-covered body.

SUMMARY

In this chapter, we witness the attempt by Godfrey's wife, Molly Farren, to revenge herself upon him. She drinks the laudanum, however, and dies in the snow. Her blond-haired baby girl, Godfrey's child, manages to escape a similar fate by entering Silas Marner's cottage and warming herself at the fire. The door is open because:

(1) Silas is hoping to see someone coming to return his stolen money.

(2) He is seized by a cataleptic attack and remains perfectly rigid until after the child has entered his house.

Observe the parallel between the loss of Silas' gold and the discovery of the golden-haired girl. Both incidents occur at night; once, the fog obscured Dunstan; now, the snow has concealed the approach of Molly Farren. In both instances, the door of Marner's cottage is open. He has had two strange occurrences in two months: in the first, he loses his golden coins; in the second, he finds a golden child.

SILAS MARNER

TEXTUAL ANALYSIS

PART ONE: CHAPTER 13

At the Red House, the party is in full pitch: the Squire is talking loudly, Dr. Kimble is absorbed in a game of cards, and the servants have come up from the kitchen to peek in at the dancers in the White Parlour. Squire Cass is praising his young son Bob for his dancing ability; Godfrey has his eyes on Nancy Lammeter. Just after Godfrey lifts his eyes away from glancing at her, he sees his own child being carried in the arms of Silas Marner! Silas has come through the door at the other end of the room. The Squire and the Rector ask Silas what is the matter; Silas tells them he has come for a doctor. The Rector wishes to know why the doctor is needed. Silas replies, "It's a woman, she's dead I think-dead in the snow at the Stone Pits-not far from my door." Nancy Lammeter asks Godfrey who the child is. Godfrey says he does not know.

Comment

In the sudden excitement, Godfrey is not sure that the child is his.

Mrs. Kimble tells Silas to leave the child at the Red House but Silas refuses; saying that the child came to him and he has a right to keep her.

Comment

Here is the first attempt by Silas to assert his right to the child. It indicates that his long dormant love for people may be ignited again by the child. Later, we shall find that further attempts will be made to separate them.

Dr. Kimble puts on his boots and sends word to have Dolly Winthrop meet him at the Stone Pits. Godfrey, determined to find out if the woman is his wife, tells the doctor he will fetch Dolly. Later, at the cottage of Silas Marner, Godfrey waits outside while Dr. Kimble and Dolly try to save Molly. Godfrey walks up and down in the snow thinking:

(1) He is afraid, if it is his wife, that everything will now be revealed to his father and Nancy,

(2) His next thought is that he should announce to everyone that he is the father of the child and to claim her from Silas Marner. However, he lacks the moral courage to perform such a actions.

(3) Finally, he judges that, if this woman were his wife and if she dies, he will finally be free to marry Nancy!

At last, Dr. Kimble comes out to announce that the woman is dead. He mentions, also, that she is wearing a wedding ring on her finger. Kimble leaves and Godfrey enters to see the dead face on the pillow. It is Molly Farren, his wife; the look on her face will haunt Godfrey for years to come. Near the fire, sits Silas Marner ... lulling the child. Godfrey asks Silas if he plans to surrender the child to the parish authorities in the village. Marner refuses; arguing that no one has a right to take the child away. "I reckon it's got no father," he tells Godfrey.

Comment

Notice the **irony** of the remark that Silas makes to Godfrey about the child not having a father.

Godfrey gives Silas some money for the child and returns to the party at the Red House. He thinks that, perhaps now, he will be able to marry Nancy for:

(1) His wife is dead.

(2) The record of his marriage will probably be forgotten; buried in the pages of a book in a distant village.

(3) He can always bribe Dunstan to remain silent if he returns.

(4) His child will be provided for; he will not forsake it.

SILAS MARNER

TEXTUAL ANALYSIS

PART ONE: CHAPTER 14

The burial of Molly Farren that week, in a pauper's grave, attracts no attention in Raveloe or in Batherly where she and her child had lived. Silas Marner's resolve to keep the child leads people to become more sympathetic towards him, although many mothers wonder how he will manage. Dolly Winthrop brings baby clothes which had been Aaron's and gives the child a bath. Dolly offers to care for the child each morning but Silas declines saying, "I want to do things for it myself, else it may get fond o'somebody else, and not fond o'me." Understanding how much Silas loves the child, Dolly tells Silas to put the clothes on the child "and then you can say you've done for her from the first of her coming to you."

Comment

Once more, Silas asserts his independence with the child although he is not unwilling to share her with others to an extent.

Dolly cautions Silas about minding the child. Silas says he will tie her to the loom with a long strip of "something" during the day when he is weaving. Mrs. Winthrop promises to bring some pieces of red cloth and other objects for her to play with. Then, she urges Silas to have the child christened. Silas does not know that christening is baptism; a religious ceremony in which the child receives a name and entrance into the church. When he finally understands, his fear of christening leaves him and he consents to have the child called Hephzibah after his younger sister (who died as a child). Dolly does not object to the name because Silas tells her it appears in the Bible but she wonders if it is not a "hard" name. Silas tells her that he called his sister "Eppie."

The child is indeed christened by the Rector. He knows that there is a chance that the child has already been christened but he judges it to be a greater risk not to baptized than to risk baptizing her twice. Silas begins to attend church again because Dolly says it is for the good of the child. Months pass and, unlike Silas' dead gold which was hidden away, Eppie loves sunshine and living things. The gold has led Silas' thoughts, in a circle, back to more thoughts of gold; Eppie now makes his thoughts move forward to the future. The gold has made Silas sit all day at his loom; Eppie calls him away to carry her to the meadows where the flowers grow. She plucks the flowers and, listens to the notes of a bird's song. Silas begins to look for herbs again as he used to do years before.

Comment

The change that Eppie brings into the life of Silas is perhaps the most important **theme** in the novel. George Eliot was very much impressed by the lines which William Wordsworth, the

Romantic poet, had written. "A child more than any of the gifts offered to declining man / Brings with it hope and forward-looking thoughts." It is apparent how the author has constructed the novel, up to this point, to show us a man (Silas Marner) who has dried up all the love in his heart. Now, however, through the effect that Eppie has upon him, his spirit will again awaken. George Eliot thought that warm, human relationships between people had a remedial effect; that is, a person whose spirit might be ill because of loss, disappointment or despair could, through the bonds of human love and affection, find hope for the future.

Dolly Winthrop, fearing that Silas is too indulgent with Eppie, suggests that she be punished when she misbehaves. She had four boys of her own and did not hesitate to make certain areas of their anatomy tingle occasionally. But Silas does not wish to hurt Eppie. Dolly tells him of how she used to lock Aaron in the coal bin for a few minutes as a disciplinary measure. One day, Silas tries to use the coal bin for Eppie. As he planned, Silas ties Eppie to his loom each morning with a strip of linen cloth. One morning, Eppie, reaching up and taking a pair of scissors, cuts herself free. Not until Silas needs his scissors does he notice that Eppie is gone! He runs from the house shouting her name. He fears she may have fallen into the stone pits. Perhaps, she has crawled through the fence and is over in the Osgoods' fields. Silas searches one meadow, crosses another fence into a second and, finally, when his hope is almost gone, he discovers Eppie by the edge of a small pond; happily playing in the mud. Silas embraces her; sobbing in relief and happiness. Upon his return to the cottage, however, he decides to punish her by putting her into the coal-hole (a small closet for fuel near the hearth). Eppie enters happily ... much to his surprise. Silas holds the door closed. All is silent until Eppie cries out, "Opy, Opy." Silas lets her out hoping that the punishment has worked. Eppie is black from the dirt in the coal hole, so Silas spends time washing and dressing her. Silas decides he will not need a new linen band with which tie her. He turns his back for a moment. Suddenly he sees Eppie, her hands and face black once more, peeping out of the coal-hole. She says, "Eppie in the coal-hole!"

Comment

In this warm, humorous scene, we find that Silas is an specially warm and kind person. We also judge that Eppie will grow up without very much punishment.

Silas takes Eppie with him whenever he goes out; they become known and liked by everyone in Raveloe. Everyone wants them to sit and talk. Much advice is given to Silas. Even children are not afraid of approaching Silas now that Eppie is with him. Silas enjoys the company, realizing that he must find out, from others, as much as he can so that he may become a better father to Eppie. She is like a plant and he must know all he can about the weather and soil so that she will grow up strong and free from harm. Silas never misses his money now; nor could he ever feels strongly about it as he did formerly, for now he has Eppie. She gives real purpose to his earnings now; hope and joy carrying him beyond any monetary thoughts.

SUMMARY

Opening on a somber note with the funeral of Molly Farren, the chapter shows, primarily, the great transformation in Silas caused by the child Eppie. Moreover, we notice:

(1) Silas has the child christened and begins to go to church again.

(2) Eppie is mischievous at times but Silas is simply unable to be severe with her. His attempt to discipline her by placing her in the coal-hole backfires. Finally he accepts the truth that she will be reared without any punishment.

At the close of the chapter, George Eliot uses a **metaphor** taken from the Bible to express part of her purpose in writing the novel. In earlier times, there were angels who came and took men by the hand and led them away from the city of destruction. Although there are no white-winged angels now, men can be led away from threatening destruction: a hand is put in theirs and leads them to a calm and bright land; the hand may be a child's. Once again, the author repeats the idea that a small child has the power to give man a sense of promise and expectation. Eppie is Silas' hope for the future.

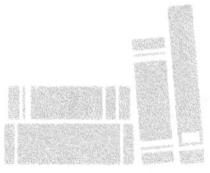

SILAS MARNER

TEXTUAL ANALYSIS

PART ONE: CHAPTER 15

....

Godfrey Cass watches, with hidden interest, the growth of his child, Eppie, under the care of the weaver. Occasionally, he gives a present to Silas but he knows he must be careful not to arouse suspicion. He does not wish people to wonder why he is interested in the welfare of a poor man and his adopted child. Godfrey does not feel uneasy about leaving his child to be reared by another. He excuses his attitude by telling himself that children brought up in humble surroundings are often happier than those brought up in luxury.

Godfrey does feel regret (but it is seldom) for now his whole attitude toward life has changed. He seems happier. Dunstan has not returned; perhaps he has joined the army and left the country. No one cares nor asks about him. Godfrey stops worrying about him. Almost every day of the week, he can be seen riding to the Warrens' house to see Nancy.

Comment

Remember that Godfrey is free to marry Nancy because his wife, Molly Farren, is dead.

Godfrey has visions of marrying Nancy and can picture himself playing with his children at the hearth. As far as Eppie is concerned, he will see that she is always provided for; but he will never reveal that she is his daughter.

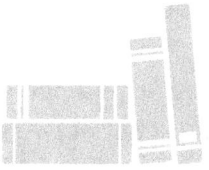

SILAS MARNER

TEXTUAL ANALYSIS

PART TWO: CHAPTER 1

....

Sixteen years have passed. Eppie is about eighteen years old and Silas is about fifty-five. It is a bright autumn Sunday in Raveloe and we see the villagers coming out of the old church across the street from the Red House. Godfrey Cass, one of the most important men in Raveloe, is among the first to leave. With him, is his pretty wife, Nancy. They have been married for fifteen years but have no children. The Squire has died and his inheritance has been divided among his sons; all except Dunstan, who has disappeared long ago. Walking behind Godfrey and Nancy are Priscilla Lammeter and her father, who is now quite aged. Priscilla never married, preferring to remain independent. They still live at their estate, the Warrens, but they are going to the Red House to have Sunday dinner with Godfrey and Nancy. Among the others in the congregation are Silas Marner and Eppie. Silas, with his white hair and stooped shoulders looks like a much older man than he actually is. Eppie is a very dainty and beautiful girl with a light complexion, curly reddish-brown hair and dimples. Walking behind Eppie is Aaron Winthrop, now a good-looking young gardener of twenty-three.

He is listening to the conversation between Eppie and Silas. Eppie tells her old father that she wishes that they had a little garden like Dolly Winthrop (Aaron's mother) has at her cottage.

Comment

The second part of the novel occurs after an extended period of time. Look for the changes in people as George Eliot describes them. We find that Godfrey Cass has married Nancy but that they have no children. The Squire is dead; Dunsey has never returned; Priscilla and her father live at the Warrens but often visit Nancy and Godfrey at the Red House. Eppie has not been claimed by Godfrey as his daughter so Silas has been her father. He has told her that he found her mother dead in the snow and that no ones knows who her real father is. Now, she is very lovely. Her suggestion that she would like a garden such as Dolly Winthrop has may be a hint that she would like to have the company of Aaron Winthrop. He would probably dig it for her.

Silas agrees to have a garden; he can dig it in the morning and in the evening when he is not working at his loom. He wonders why Eppie has not mentioned this to him before. Suddenly, Aaron comes forward and exclaims that he can dig the garden instead of Silas. He will be able to find time during the slack in work at the Red House where he is Godfrey Cass' gardener; or else after work. He tells Silas that he will ask to bring soil from Godfrey's garden, also. Eppie tells Silas that he should do only the light work in the garden with her; she plans to have rosemary, bergamot and thyme. Aaron tells her, he will bring lavender from Godfrey's garden. She says she thinks: "The flowers can see us and know what we're talking about." Silas does not want to ask for anything more from Mr. Cass because Godfrey has already been very generous to him and Eppie; building a new addition to their cottage. Aaron explains that the flowers can easily be spared and he observes that, if all good farming land was used, for example, no one need go hungry in the world. Eppie asks Aaron to bring Dolly to the stone pits, also, because she can advise them about the garden. Aaron leaves. Eppie happily skips for she knows that Aaron likes her and that he will dig the garden for her. Silas and Eppie are greeted by one of their donkeys as they approach their cottage at the stone pits.

Inside, they are met by their brown terrier, Snap. A cat and a kitten are their other pets. The beautiful oak furniture in their cottage is the gift of Godfrey Cass. Eppie prepares their Sunday meal and Silas watches as she feeds the animals. Later, he goes outside to smoke. Silas has begun smoking for the past two years on the advice of the so-called wise men of the village. (Mr. Macey is still giving advice at eighty six. He predicts that Silas will someday have his money returned.)

Comment

Silas and Eppie live a quiet and simple life. Together, they have happily passed the years with their friends and their pets. The author now employs a summary of what has occurred during the past sixteen years as far as certain attitudes of Silas are concerned.

Silas smokes a pipe because other people in Raveloe advise him to do so. Through force of habit, Silas has become used to following the advice of his neighbors because, when he first found Eppie on his hearth years before, he knew the only way he could manage was to listen to what others told him about what to do for her. He began to trust in his neighbors; wondering if, perhaps, there might have been some error in his thinking, as a young man, when he lost his faith in God and Man after the drawing of the lots which had found him guilty of the robbery at Lantern Yard. Over the years, he had gradually revealed to Dolly Winthrop the circumstances of his early life. Dolly did not understand quickly, needing repeated explanations of what happened before she comprehended the absurd plan of drawing the lots to find if Silas were guilty or innocent. She thought, perhaps, that Silas belonged to a totally different kind of religion but Silas assured her that he used the same Bible at lantern Yard that Dolly used. Dolly was confused and, although admitting that she did not have the power to understand it as well as "wise folks" like the parson might, she told Silas that if "Them above" (God) had been fair to Silas, he would have been found innocent. Silas explained to Dolly that, because he was found guilty and his friend William Dane had "framed" him, he lost his faith. Dolly said Dane was truly a "bad 'un" and brought up the subject of the lots again. This time, she said that those who drew the lots (except for William Dane) probably thought they had done the right thing but God knew the truth of Silas' innocence, regardless of their verdict. Dolly admitted that suffering and pain come into the world and many things occur which can never be satisfactorily explained but she concluded: "all as we've got to do is trusten, Master Marner-to do the right thing as far as we know, and to trusten." If Silas could have gone on trusting in God after he had been so disappointed, he might never have run away from his fellow human beings and become so lonely. Silas agreed that trusting would have been difficult but that it would have been "right." He recognized now that there was good in the world along with the evil. The drawing of the lots was "dark," but Eppie was sent to him, so there is a certain kind of justice: "there's dealings with us-there's dealings."

> Comment

By talking to Dolly Winthrop about his past, Silas has been able to see the reasons why he gave up hope and why it was a mistake to judge God and all human beings so harshly because of the plotting of William Dane and the misguided judgment of his Lantern Yard brethren.

Silas had also often talked to Eppie about the past. This was when she became mature enough to understand. He did not wish her to find out about her past through the gossip of Raveloe neighbors. Eppie was told about how her mother had died on the snowy ground and how she herself had been found on the hearth by Silas-who had mistaken her golden curls for his gold.

Eppie had not even thought about her real father until the day Silas gave her the wedding ring which had been taken from the wasted finger of Molly Farren. She kept it in a small shoe-shaped box and, when she looked at it, she did not think of her father but of her mother. She often asked Silas how she looked and whom she was like.

> Comment

Silas has wisely told Eppie about her past. She feels no love for any father but often asks Silas about her dead mother. Both she and Silas do not realize, of course, that Godfrey is her true father.

On that same Sunday (sixteen years later) Eppie joins Silas. He is now outside of the cottage smoking his pipe. Eppie asks Silas if they can transplant (to the new garden) the furze bush on which Molly Farren, her mother, had lain the night she died.

Silas agrees; also suggesting that a fence must be erected to prevent their donkeys and the other animals from trampling everything in the garden. Since a fence, however, is an expensive item, Eppie suggests that a wall of stones be built instead. Silas and Aaron can gather the larger stones and she the smaller ones. To demonstrate her rock-carrying ability, Eppie skips over to the stone pits, then calls to Silas, "O father, come and see how the water's gone down since yesterday. Why, yesterday, the pit was ever so full!" Silas explains that the pit is being drained so that the water may be transferred to Mr. Osgood's field, which is next to Silas' cottage and has now been taken over by Godfrey Cass.

Comment

The draining of the stone pits is a significant incident for it will change the lives of Godfrey, Nancy, Silas, and Eppie.

Eppie, sitting on a bank with Silas in the shadows of the late afternoon, suggests gently that she has been thinking of marrying. She introduces this thought by asking Silas if she should wear her mother's wedding ring if she ever marries. Silas has thought that someday she might marry and he now asks her if Aaron wants to marry her. Hoping Silas will consent, Eppie admits it; telling Silas that she is in love with him and that he is prospering as a gardener with work at the Red House, Mr. Osgood's, and soon, at the Rectory. Eppie explains that both Aaron and she would expect Silas to live with them after they are married. Eppie has told Aaron that she is happy with her present life and Aaron has made her cry by telling her that if she really loves him she would marry him.

Comment

Eppie is faced with a problem of divided love:

(1) She loves Silas; yet, she wishes to marry Aaron.

(2) Eppie's love for Aaron is strong but her love for Silas makes her want to stay with him; even though Aaron has shown his love for the weaver by wanting him to live with them after they are married. Eppie is hoping, primarily, that Silas will accept Aaron as her husband and consent to live with them.

Silas lays down his pipe; saying that Eppie is "young to get married." He suggests that Mrs. Winthrop be asked for her opinion. Yet, Silas recognizes that things do change in life; someday, he will be older and more helpless. He has thought that it would be a comforting thing to know that someone young and strong would then be able to care for Eppie. "Then, would you like me to be married, father?" Eppie asks, with a little trembling in her voice. Silas tells her he will consent to her marriage but that Dolly Winthrop, Eppie's godmother at her baptism, must also consent. Just then, Eppie sees Dolly and Aaron coming to the cottage.

SUMMARY

In this long first chapter of the second part of the novel we discover that sixteen years have elapsed since the night that Silas first discovered Eppie. Several important developments have occurred in this long passage of time:

(1) Godfrey has married Nancy. His first marriage is still a secret. No one ever discovered that he had been married to Molly Farren, the unidentified woman found in the snow.

(2) Silas has become the only father Eppie has ever known although her true father, Godfrey, has helped her and Silas financially through the years.

(3) Dunsey Cass has never returned. His whereabouts are unknown. Later in the chapter, we find that Eppie wishes to build a garden and that Aaron Winthrop (who once came to visit Silas with his mother shortly after the robbery) is the man she loves. Eppie reveals her love for Aaron to her father. We also perceive, in this chapter, an attempt by Dolly Winthrop to explain the reasons for Marner's loss of faith to him. She tells him, essentially, that his mistake is to blame God and all men for the willful plotting of William Dane and the poor judgment of the others in choosing lots to find Silas guilty. Silas realizes, as Dolly points out, that the important thing to do in times of great disappointment and loss, is "to trusten"; to have faith in God. One new incident, which will become significant, is the draining of water from the stone pits.

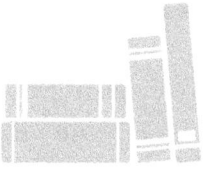

SILAS MARNER

TEXTUAL ANALYSIS

PART TWO: CHAPTER 2

....

Meanwhile, at the Red House on the same Sunday afternoon, Priscilla Lammeter and her father are preparing to leave for their home after having dinner with Nancy and Godfrey. The parlour of the Red House has changed since the days when Squire Cass was alive.

(1) Everything is now polished and is dusted every day.

(2) All sporting equipment, guns, whips, etc., have been carefully hung on the antlers of a stuffed stag over the fireplace. The tankards gleam untouched because they are always empty.

(3) The smell of stale ale has been replaced by lavender and rose-leaves.

All has been purity and order in the Red House since Godfrey married Nancy, fifteen years ago. Nancy asks her father to stay but he permits Priscilla to answer for him since she "manages" him and his business on the farm. This because of his advanced age. Priscilla wishes to leave, without staying for tea, because she must return to the Warrens to be certain that one of their dairymaids (who is soon to be married) performs her tasks properly. As the horses are being readied, Priscilla tells Nancy that she is glad that Godfrey had decided to enter the dairy business; for it will keep her occupied and free from melancholy thoughts.

Comment

Priscilla knows that Nancy and Godfrey are disappointed because they have had no children.

Priscilla knows that Godfrey also has been restless because they are childless and suggests to Nancy that she could have remained single. Nancy defends Godfrey by saying it is natural that Godfrey should be disappointed; otherwise, "He's the best of husbands." The gig (carriage) approaches. It is drawn by the Lammeter's horse, Speckle, and Priscilla leaves with her father. Nancy begins to read her Bible while Godfrey goes for his accustomed Sunday afternoon walk. Alone with her thoughts about her life with Godfrey, Nancy feels that Godfrey suffers because they have had no children much more than she does. Nancy had lost a baby early in their marriage and, although she still has a drawer full of baby clothes, all unworn, she refuses to permit herself to complain about the baby's death. She never opens the drawer for she feels she would be wishing for something that was not meant to happen. She wonders now if she has done the right thing for Godfrey by refusing, six years ago, to adopt Eppie.

Comment

There are four reasons why Nancy did not wish to adopt a child:

(1) People in the early nineteenth century were less ready to rear children who were not their own than people are today. Adoption was a much rarer practice then than it is now.

(2) Nancy felt that it would be against the will of Providence to have children if they were not their own.

(3) Because of her rigid code and inflexible nature, once Nancy had determined upon a course of action, she would not change. We recall how strictly she adhered to her habits: years earlier, at the dance at the Red House, she insisted upon wearing the same kind of dress as Priscilla because "it was right for sisters to dress alike." Nancy is meticulous in her dress and personal belongings. Every article in her home is in its proper place. Her lack of deviation from a fixed or ordered pattern causes her to become rigid in her opinions. She thinks it wrong to adopt a child because God did not give her one; she will continue to think that way.

(4) Nancy is somewhat superstitious. For example, she would not make a purchase at a particular place if, on three successive occasions, rain or some obstacle had prevented her from going. She views such happenings as warnings from heaven.

This last reason of Nancy's is commented upon by George Eliot (who was not a member of a formal religion) as an instance of how human belief can arrive at a truth akin to a belief which is theological. In other words, the author is saying that ideas of a human can equal the ideas of a religion. One belief comes from man; the other from God. We may infer that the author does not believe in the supernatural dogma of Christianity.

Years earlier, when Eppie was about twelve, Godfrey had told Nancy that he wanted to adopt her (never realizing how Silas and Eppie felt about each other!) Nancy had refused, hoping that he would understand. Godfrey admired Nancy for the strength of her conviction concerning Eppie and, although he was disappointed, he accepted it. Naturally, he knew that he could never tell Nancy that Eppie was his own child and he felt that their childless state now was more or less a retribution for his abandonment of her to Silas when she was a child.

Nancy, sitting alone, wonders how lonely Godfrey would be if she died. Suddenly, a servant (Jane) informs her mistress that she has seen a number of people "making haste" down the road; she ends by saying, "I hope nobody's been hurt that's all." Nancy, wishing that Jane would not terrify her so, thinks that perhaps a bull has broken loose. She walks to the window and gazes out; hoping for Godfrey's return, yet, sensing a strange fear.

SUMMARY

We find that Nancy and Godfrey cannot find complete marital happiness because they have no children. Nancy is resigned to this truth because she accepts it as God's will but Godfrey is restless. Their first child died and, later, Nancy refused to adopt Eppie because of her rigid opinions. Godfrey began to see his childless marriage as retribution for his permitting Silas to rear Eppie; his own child.

SILAS MARNER

TEXTUAL ANALYSIS

PART TWO: CHAPTER 3

Just then, the door opens and Godfrey enters. He is pale and motions Nancy to be seated. Jane leaves the room and the trembling Godfrey begins to speak: "I've had a great shock." Nancy becomes frightened; fearing that something has happened to her father and Priscilla. Godfrey answers, "It's Dunstan - my brother . . . we've found him - found his body - his skeleton." Nancy feels somewhat relieved open hearing that the news was not about her father and Priscilla. Godfrey explains that the stone pit has suddenly gone dry. This was probably from draining it for the land Godfrey had bought from Mr. Osgood for his future dairy farm. Dunstan's body has lain for sixteen years, wedged tightly between two great stones. This prevented him from saving himself. His watch and Godfrey's gold-handled riding whip, which Dunstan had borrowed the day he went to sell Wildfire, are found. The name Godfrey Cass is inscribed on the handle of the whip. Godfrey pauses. Nancy asks if Dunstan had drowned himself. "No, he fell in," Godfrey answers, adding, "Dunstan was the man that robbed Silas Marner." Nancy blushes, ashamed at the dishonor she feels. She sympathizes for Godfrey who continues by explaining that the money which Dunstan had stolen from the cottage of Silas Marner also has been found.

Comment

We learn that several significant facts are discovered by Godfrey and Nancy in this chapter:

(1) Dunsey is dead.

(2) He is the thief who stole Marner's money.

(3) Silas' money has been found. His fortune will be returned to him.

Nancy senses that Godfrey has something else to tell her: Godfrey admits that he has been living with a secret on his mind for years but, now, he will tell her. Nancy is frightened again. Godfrey reveals that the woman Silas found dead in the snow, "Eppie's mother-that wretched woman-was my wife: Eppie is my child." Nancy is silent. Godfrey tries to defend himself. He explains that he knew he should not have left the child unowned yet he was afraid to tell Nancy earlier because he might lose her. Nancy looks at Godfrey and answers regretfully that, if he had only told her that Eppie was his child six years ago, they could have done their duty by her. "Do you think I'd have refused to take her in knowing she was yours?" Nancy asks. She tells Godfrey she would have taken Eppie in as a baby and cared for her as her own child. It would have been easier for her to bear the loss of her own baby and both she and Godfrey would have been happier in their marriage.

Comment

It is ironic that, when Godfrey finally reveals the secret marriage which he hesitated to do for years (because he feared losing Nancy), he finds, contrary to his expectation, that she would have welcomed the child. Here is an example of Godfrey's inability to understand the true worth of his wife. His error in judgment has resulted in two bitter consequences:

(1) The secret about Eppie was discovered eventually although he concealed it.

(2) Because he concealed it, Nancy did not know that Eppie was his child and refused to adopt her. Thus, both of them lost years of happiness with her.

Nancy begins to cry. Godfrey attempts to depend his action explaining to Nancy that he was afraid to tell her years earlier because of her pride and her father's great pride; she would have hated him. Nancy admits to Godfrey that she doesn't know what she would have done but she wouldn't have married anyone else. She adds: "But I wasn't worth doing wrong for-nothing is in this world." Nancy smiles sadly admitting that even their marriage was not as good as Godfrey had expected it would be. Nancy feels that the person most injured is Eppie; both agree to adopt her into their home. Plans are made to visit Silas Marner's house as soon as everything is quiet down at the stone pits.

SUMMARY

In this brief, but revelatory chapter, much light is shed on past events and much speculation is created about the future. The disappearance of Dunsey Cass is finally explained;

Marner is a rich man again; Godfrey has at last revealed his two-fold secret:

(1) His marriage to Molly Farren, the woman found dead at the Stone Pits.

(2) Eppie is his child.

Nancy is shocked and disappointed; she tells Godfrey that she would have agreed to adopt Eppie if she had only known that she was Godfrey's child. She senses that their marriage has not been as happy as it could have been. We wonder what the reaction of Marner and Eppie will be, now that Nancy and Godfrey have decided to adopt Eppie.

SILAS MARNER

TEXTUAL ANALYSIS

PART TWO: CHAPTER 4

In Silas Marner's cottage that night, he and Eppie are discussing the events of the day. Aaron and his mother, Mrs. Winthrop, are the last people to leave after the excitement of discovering Dunsey Cass' body and Silas' gold. Numerous people were into the cottage; now, Silas and Eppie are alone. The gold is arranged in orderly heaps on a table. Silas has been sitting in the candlelight, telling Eppie of how he used to count it every night and how desolate he was until she was "sent" to him; he explains how much she came to mean to him. Eppie says, "If it hadn't been for you, they'd have taken me to the workhouse and there's been nobody to love me." Silas sits in silence for a few minutes looking at the money and wondering if it ever could "take a hold" of him again. Silas is afraid that, if he lost Eppie, he might think that he was forsaken again and lose the feeling that God was good to him.

Comment

The discovery of the gold causes Silas to consider his values. Never can the money replace the happiness Silas has found with Eppie. Yet, he fears that, if he should ever lose Eppie, he might return to his eccentric habits of counting it each night.

Just then, there is a knocking at the door. Eppie opens the door to Mr. and Mrs. Godfrey Cass and curtsies to them as they enter. Nancy apologizes for coming so late. (It is between eight and nine o'clock.) She and Godfrey sit opposite Silas and Eppie. Uneasily, Godfrey begins to explain why he and his wife have come to visit. He tells Silas that it is a comfort to him to see the money returned; especially since someone in his family had stolen it. He almost blurts out that he is also indebted to Silas for caring for his child, Eppie, but he and Nancy had agreed that the secret of her real fatherhood should not be disclosed to Eppie, if possible, until the future. Godfrey suggests to Silas that he is growing older (Silas admits he is fifty-five) and since, after all, the money was returned to him but couldn't last forever, perhaps he would like to see Eppie well provided for. Godfrey is clearly expressing a wish to take Eppie into his family and to have her live at the Red House. Silas, however, is unsure of Godfrey's intention. "I don't take your meaning, sir" he answers.

Godfrey explains that he and his wife would like to have Eppie as their daughter. While he is speaking, Eppie slips her hand behind her father's head; Silas is trembling. When Godfrey finishes, Silas speaks to Eppie, telling her that he "won't stand in her way" if she wishes to go to live with Mr. and Mrs. Cass.

Eppie gives a low courtesy and thanks Godfrey and Nancy telling them, "I can't leave my father." She adds, "I don't want to be a lady-thank you all the same." She retreats to her father's chair and puts her hand around his neck.

Godfrey finally admits, in desperation, that he is Eppie's father. "She's my own child: her mother was my wife." Godfrey feels that his natural claim on his daughter supercedes all others.

Comment

Notice how Godfrey fails to appreciate other people's feelings. He does not realize how much suffering Silas would experience if Eppie were to leave him.

Silas demands bitterly to know why Godfrey did not admit his fatherhood sixteen years earlier before he (Silas) had come to love her. He tells Godfrey that God gave Eppie to him because Godfrey had turned his back on her. He then concludes by observing: "When a man turns a blessing from his door, it falls to them as take it in."

Comment

Here is another **theme** which echoes the adage about opportunity knocking but once.

Godfrey admits that he was wrong but defends his position by saying he has repented of his earlier refusal to accept and acknowledge Eppie. Silas refuses to accept mere repentance because it doesn't "alter the feelings inside us." Godfrey is awed at the truth of Silas' words but continues his plea for Eppie. Silas refuses again. Godfrey is becoming angry slowly. He begins to assert his authority; accusing Silas of standing in the way of

Eppie's welfare. He concludes that it is his "duty" to insist on taking care of his own daughter.

Eppie is thinking of her past life with Silas and what a future life with Godfrey as her father would be like. She is repelled by the thought of accepting Godfrey's offer. Silas, on the other hand, is unsure in his conscience. Is he actually retarding the way of Eppie's happiness? Finally he speaks, saying that he will leave the decision to Eppie, "I'll hinder nothing."

Nancy breathes a sigh of relief, assuming that any poor person like Eppie would naturally be anxious to receive the benefits of a wealthier life. She feels as Godfrey does; that their wish is achieved. Both of them tell Eppie how much she will mean to them. "You'll be a treasure to me," Nancy tells her.

Once more, Eppie steps forward to curtsy. After thanking them again, Eppie then speaks with a colder decision than previously. She utterly refuses to leave her father; explaining that, without him, she could never be happy. Silas has loved her from the first and nobody shall ever come between them. Silas asks Eppie to be sure; she replies that she can never be sorry because she never cared for the "fine things" such as clothes, a carriage, or a place in church (a special, reserved pew).

Nancy, seeing that Godfrey has no reply, cautions Eppie that she should accept the offer of her lawful father; but Eppie, her eyes welling with tears, disagrees about the idea and tells her that the only "father" she believes she ever had is Silas. In the midst of tears, Eppie reveals her strong love for "a workingman" and her engagement to him.

Godfrey's face is flushed and he is unable to say anything but "Let us go!" Nancy suggests that they will come and visit again.

SUMMARY

The attempts of Godfrey and Nancy to win Eppie are fruitless. They present several reasons to Silas why Eppie should come:

(1) Godfrey and Nancy have no children and would like to rear Eppie. This reason, however, is rejected. Godfrey therefore argues:

(2) He is the real father of Eppie and has a claim over her. Silas refuses to accept the validity of such a claim because Godfrey has neglected the child for sixteen years. Godfrey appeals to Silas and Eppie on the grounds that:

(3) He can give advantages which only a wealthy girl can have. Silas is ready to admit this truth leaving the decision to Eppie; She decisively rejects the offer because:

(4) She is unaccustomed to luxuries.

(5) She is engaged to be married to a workingman. (She does not specify Aaron by name.)

SILAS MARNER

TEXTUAL ANALYSIS

PART TWO: CHAPTERS 5 AND 6

....

PART TWO, CHAPTER FIVE

Nancy and Godfrey walk home in the starlight. When they enter the Red House, Godfrey sits in a chair and says "That's ended." Nancy agrees; it would be wrong for them to force Eppie to come against her will. Godfrey sadly remembers what Silas said about a man's turning a blessing from his door: it falls to somebody else. Nancy asks Godfrey if he will make it known that Eppie is his daughter but Godfrey refuses; judging that no possible good can come from such a revelation. He is more concerned with helping her after her marriage; he guesses correctly that she is probably in love with Aaron for he remembers seeing them come out of church together.

Nancy is relieved that her sister Priscilla and her father will never learn of Eppie's real father. She also observes that Aaron is a sober and industrious person. Godfrey determines to leave all the information in his will. He feels sorrow that his daughter disliked him; yet, he accepts it as part of his punishment for his shirking of his duty to her. Nancy tacitly agrees. Her spirit of righteousness does not permit her to soften the edge of what she feels is proper remorse. Nancy asks Godfrey to become resigned to this which is their lot in life. Godfrey agrees it may not be too late to learn to accept the way things are but he does regret that it is too late to mend "some" things.

Comment

The **theme** of this chapter is acceptance. Godfrey and Nancy, after returning home and considering the refusal of Eppie to become their charge, learn to accept her decision. Godfrey will keep his parenthood a secret until he dies. Both he and Nancy can accept Aaron as her husband. Together, they will live out their lives without children; hoping to help Eppie when they can but realizing that it is too late to change the truth of Godfrey's earlier treatment of her.

PART TWO, CHAPTER SIX

The next morning, at breakfast, Silas suggests to Eppie that they set out the following day on a journey to Lantern Yard where Silas had been accused of the theft of the dead Deacon's money. Silas wishes:

(1) to discover if any proof of his innocence has been discovered.

(2) to speak to a Mr. Paston (who was the minister) about the drawing of the lots.

(3) to discuss the religion of the people who live in the country-side people like those in Raveloe.

Eppie is happy to go so that she can recount the trip to Aaron; since he seems to know so much about things. She considers it a small "advantage" that she will be able to tell him something. Mrs. Winthrop, assured that the journey will not be a perilous one, is well pleased that Silas should visit his native place to find out if he has been finally cleared of the mistaken guilt for the robbery.

Four days later, Silas and Eppie are walking in the streets of a large manufacturing town; looking for that section of the town called Lantern Yard. Eppie, seeing a gentleman standing in a doorway, asks Silas to inquire from him the directions to Lantern Yard but Silas refuses stating that the gentlemen of the town would not know of its existence. Silas does receive directions to the jail, however, and he and Eppie proceed to turn left three blocks past it. After a few more turns, they come to Shoe Lane and proceed to a street near an overhanging window.

All the while they have been walking, Eppie and her father have been shocked by the dreary aspect of the town. Eppie calls it a "dark, ugly" place. She is "stifled" by the way the people live so closely together and thinks of how delightful it will be to return to the Stone Pits. Even Silas notices a change. The air smells bad but it "usened" (used) to smell differently years before. Occasionally, a grimy face peers at them from a doorway; such glances only increase Eppie's uneasiness.

Suddenly, Silas stops short; there is an amazed look on his face. They are standing before the exit of a large factory through which men and women are hurrying on their way to lunch. Finally, Silas says, "It's gone, child. Lantern Yard's gone." Indeed, a large factory has replaced the area in which the chapel, the graveyard, and the buildings where Lantern Yard stood had been. Eppie, afraid that Silas may suffer one of his cataleptic attacks, leads him to a little brush shop so that he may sit down. However, no one can tell Marner anything more than that the factory was ten years old; nothing is known of any of his old friends or of Mr. Paston the minister.

When Silas and Eppie return to Raveloe, Silas tells Dolly Winthrop that, now, he will never know whether Mr. Paston could have given him any information about the drawing of the lots. Marner is resigned to the probability that it will remain "dark to the last"; that is, until he dies. Dolly agrees observing that "them above" (God) have many things they prefer should remain "dark" to men. The simple things in living and the daily tasks she faces are the aspects of life which Dolly understands: "mostly what comes i' the day's work." She concludes that Silas was unjustly treated once and, to be sure, he will never know the reason for it; yet, that does not hinder there being a reason for it even if "it's all dark" or incapable of being understood. Silas agrees with Dolly saying that, since Eppie has come to him, he has had enough light to "trusten by" (hope in God) and, now that Eppie has told him that he will live with her and Aaron after they are married, Silas believes he will "trusten" until he dies.

SUMMARY

Over thirty years have elapsed since Silas left Lantern Yard. George Eliot pictures his return in a manner which echoes Washington Irving's Rip Van Winkle. Both men return to their former villages (decades after leaving them) to be greeted with numerous changes. England, at the time of Silas and Eppie, was undergoing the beginning of a vast number of technological and social changes caused by the first rumblings of the industrial revolution of the nineteenth century. Compare this chapter with the first to see how the author expresses the differences in life for men at the beginning of the century, "when spinning wheels hummed busily" with the great changes wrought by machines a mere thirty years later. The city is beginning to replace the country as a home for most men; the skilled worker, with his craft and pride in creating excellence in his products, is disappearing; his son is probably working long hours in a large brick factory performing a routine, unchallenging job in a mass-producing business.

Silas is lost in such a world and he returns gratefully to Raveloe. Although he has not been successful in determining anything new about his past experience at Lantern Yard, he reveals (in his discussion with Dolly Winthrop) an acceptance of life's mysteries; we notice that this acceptance **theme** had a parallel in the previous chapter as Godfrey and Nancy agreed to face their future without hope of having Eppie.

CONCLUSION

Springtime in Raveloe was always considered an especially appropriate time for a wedding. The ornamental flowers, such as the yellow laburnum shrubs and the April lilacs, are blowing. Eppie is seen going by the Red House and into the church with one arm on Aaron; the other is on her father. She is wearing a light, white cotton dress with a pink sprig at the side; the gown is a gift from Mrs. Cass. Her hair looks as if it is the dash of gold found on a lily. Miss Priscilla Lammeter and her father pull up in their carriage just in time to see the bridal party, which also includes Ben and Dolly Winthrop who enter the church. Priscilla and her father agree it is unfortunate that Nancy never had a child. Just then Nancy comes out and Priscilla and her father meet her. Neither Nancy or Godfrey attend the ceremony. Godfrey is out of town on "business" in Lytherly but he has ordered a wedding feast for the bridal party and the townspeople at the Rainbow Tavern.

As the wedding party passes Mr. Macey (who is sitting outside his own door in an armchair) they stop on the advice of Dolly who knows he is too old to attend the wedding feast. Mr. Macey has a few things to say to Silas; chiefly that he has lived to see his prediction come true that Silas would receive his money again.

In the open yard of the Rainbow Tavern, the guests have assembled although it is still nearly an hour before the wedding reception. The men are discussing Silas Marner's strange story and even Mr. Snell, the farrier (veterinary), agrees that Silas had "brought a blessing upon himself" by adopting and rearing Eppie, an orphaned child. Suddenly, the bridal group is seen approaching the Rainbow and a cheer is given by those assembled there. Ben Winthrop runs out of the bridal party which is coming from the church to the Stone Pits for an hour of quiet before the reception. He shakes hands briefly and exchanges congratulations with the men at the tavern.

Eppie, Aaron, Silas, and Dolly approach the Stone Pits, which will be the new home of Eppie, her husband, and her father. Eppie joyfully exclaims that no one could have been happier than they are!

SUMMARY

The conclusion (although considered by some readers to be unnecessary to the story because it is to be assumed that all will end happily for Silas and Eppie) is nevertheless a pleasant and warm picture of a springtime wedding in rural England.

An interesting insight into how Godfrey and Nancy have decided to act towards Eppie is shown in their refusal to attend the wedding although Nancy has donated the dress and Godfrey has financed the wedding feast. Nancy invites her father and sister to visit so that she cannot attend; it is deliberately arranged for Godfrey to be unavailable at the marriage because of business.

SILAS MARNER

CHARACTER ANALYSES

Silas Marner

Silas Marner, the weaver of Raveloe, represents a kind of craftsman commonly seen in England in the years before the Industrial Revolution. Naturally honest and shy as a young man, Silas finds delight in the friendships he makes in the Lantern Yard church. His sincerity wins the love of Sarah and of his friend William Dane. Because he is a very thorough person, his mental processes appear to be slower than normal, yet, he is able to perceive the plot of Dane against him. His uneducated mind, surrounded by the superstitious aura, does prevent him, however, from interpreting accurately the significance of the drawing of the lots.

Through the loss of faith following his "trial," Silas becomes a cold, distant hermit; submerging those aspects of his nature which companionship had brought to the surface. Perhaps his unrelenting industry is the only one of his traits which endures: through it, and a new trait (avarice), he is able to amass a fortune in savings from weaving. His love of people has been transferred to gold. After the loss of his money, he is compelled to ask his neighbors for assistance; such contacts are multiplied and intensified when he becomes the guardian of Eppie.

Silas indicates strength of character by refusing to part with Eppie when he finds her and when, years later, he is ordered to do so by Godfrey. Although physically a wan, short-sighted man, prone to violent and prolonged cataleptic seizures which make his body rigidly motionless, Silas displays a spiritual inflexibility in his sense of justice and determination to protect Eppie, whose love had unlocked his natural emotions.

Godfrey Cass

Born into wealth, Godfrey Cass loses his mother early in his life and receives no moral guidance from his father, the Squire. Free to idle, he acquires debilitating habits and an irregular, purposeless life. Naturally generous and sincere, he lacks the moral strength to resist the influence of his dissolute younger brother, Dunstan Cass, and is led into a demeaning marriage.

His vacillation is, in part, prompted by fear and, in part, by an unrealistic, inane trust in chance. He remains silent when his wife, Molly Farren, dies and fails to acknowledge Eppie as his child; he justifies his need for future happiness as a reason for denying his child's right to parenthood.

His marriage to Nancy suddenly ends his profligacy; he now leads a correct moral life. His happiness is impaired by the loss of his only child; but it is not until Dunstan's body is discovered that he is prompted to reveal to his wife his relationship to Eppie. When Marner and his daughter refuse what he considers his lawful and magnanimous proposal, to take the child he is chagrined; yet, in time, he accepts the disappointment as a nemesis for his early indifference. That he **refrains** from attending the wedding feast indicates that he has been considerate enough to avoid Eppie the day of the wedding lest his presence mar her happiness.

William Dane

William Dane is, like Silas, a weaver; he also attends Lantern Yard church and is secretly in love with Silas' fiancée, Sarah. A naturally ambitious and proud man, Dane has predicted his own salvation by reading in a Bible, (he tells his brethren) the words "calling and election sure." His problem is to separate Sarah from Silas. We know that Silas innocently invites him to accompany him on his Sunday walks with Sarah. Dane bides his time until an appropriate situation presents itself. When the minister dies, and he arrives to find Silas in a cataleptic attack, a thought occurs to him: now, he can damage Silas' reputation permanently. He steals the money in the drawer, leaves the knife Silas has given him; to implicate Silas. He then hurries to plant the empty money box in Silas' room. Later, his treacherous advice to Silas is that he "confess." Success comes to him: he later marries Sarah. To win her, he has had only to steal, slander, and destroy the happiness of his friend: Silas Marner.

Nancy Lammeter

The younger daughter of the sober, exemplary widower, Mr. Lammeter, Nancy has a sense of family and propriety characteristic of proper young women in smaller towns. Severe in her own moral code, she could hardly be expected to condone the unstable conduct of a young man unless, of course, he happened to be Mr. Godfrey Cass and she was in love with him.

Because Nancy is dignified, reserved, and cautious, Godfrey is hesitant to tell her of his secret marriage. Yet, he knows that she alone can make him happy: she is beautiful, warm, a meticulous housekeeper and will make an exceptional mother. Refined, although she lacks formal cultural attainments, her acceptance of her childless marriage is a result of her childlike superstition and her inflexible religious scruples.

Squire Cass

The Squire is a caricature of a familiar English type: the man of influence in a small village who owes his position more to recognized heredity, wealth and name than to his own accomplishments. He lacks the warmth and humor of the gentle, model types which Addison and Steel had attempted to create as a model in their eighteenth century periodicals. Nor is the Squire the amiable Pickwick type as envisioned by Dickens. Excessive, intemperate and an ill-humored man, his occasional high spirits are merely indicative of his basically irresponsible nature.

Eppie

The true daughter of Godfrey Cass by his first marriage with Molly Warren, Eppie is a beautiful blonde child capable of great affection. She remains loyal to Silas when Godfrey and Nancy wish her to leave him for a wealthier life. A lover of nature, she delights in animals and flowers. Her sheltered, simple life promises to be even happier in her marriage to Aaron Winthrop. Her courage is shown in the crucial scene in which she refuses to recognize Godfrey's rights to her when he and Nancy come to Marner's cottage to claim her.

Priscilla Lammeter

As the older sister of Nancy, she is used as a foil to contrast with Nancy. Naturally plain, she is unconcerned with love or beauty. Utterly candid about herself and her looks. Priscilla believes it is better to be independent than married. Loyal to her father throughout his old age, she is also a shrewd and serious business manager of his estate. Basically a strong and direct person, she understands others only in the most general ways; the humor of her character arises from her complete disregard for the sensitivity of others.

Dolly Winthrop

She is the simple but kindly wife of the wheelwright, Ben Winthrop, and the mother of Eppie's future husband, Aaron. Dolly's kindness for others is her chief virtue. She befriends Silas, after his discovery of Eppie, and teaches him the proper ways to dress and feed her. Moreover, her missionary spirit results in a return to religion for Silas. Optimistic, patient, altruistic, and religious, her strongest concern and best talent is for helping others when they are in distress.

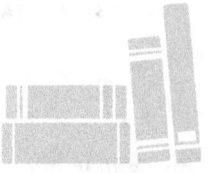

SILAS MARNER

ESSAY QUESTIONS AND ANSWERS

Question: What is the **theme** of the novel?

Answer: In *Silas Marner*, the purpose which George Eliot had in writing the work was to show how natural, human influences could remedy a damaged personality. This remedial effect which human affection creates was one of the ideas she borrowed from the Romantic poet, William Wordsworth. He expressed the thought that a child, more than any other thing which an aging man may love, brings with it "hope and forward looking thoughts." Silas Marner is returned to hopeful life through the love he gives and receives from the child, Eppie.

Question: Why is there a double metamorphosis in *Silas Marner*?

Answer: The first metamorphosis or change in Silas occurs in Lantern Yard. He loses his faith in God and his fellow human beings when he is "framed" unjustly by William Dane and then found guilty through the superstitious irrational method of choosing lots. Comparing him to a spider, the author shows him working at his loom; content to live a lone existence in which a love of gold has replaced human and divine love. The second great change in Silas occurs fifteen years after his arrival in Raveloe. The loss of his gold and the discovery of Eppie force him to seek assistance from his neighbors. They begin to express interest in him and the child; many of them become anxious to help. The presence of the child in his home rekindles Silas' love which his experience at Lantern Yard had extinguished long ago. A second transformation occurs as Silas returns slowly to his original belief and hope in God and man.

Question: What are the major strengths and weaknesses of the novel?

Answer: Foremost, perhaps, of the major attributes of *Silas Marner* is the realistic picture it leaves of nineteenth-century English country life. Other considerations include:

(1) An ingenious and complex double plot structure in which the stories of the two **protagonist**, Godfrey and Silas, are balanced without mere imitation. Both are deceived by unscrupulous men: one a friend, the other a brother. Their separate stories are united twice by incidents which force them to make decisions of far-reaching effect. When Eppie is found on his doorstep, Silas decides to keep her; Godfrey chooses to ignore his responsibility to her so that he may marry Nancy. Fourteen years later, the discovery of Dunstan Cass' skeleton prompts Godfrey to reveal his relationship to the child. (See diagram for outline of the plot.)

(2) The characterizations of Silas, Godfrey Cass, Nancy, Dunsey, the Squire, Priscilla, and the gallery of village types in early nineteenth-century England is credible throughout the work.

(3) The ethical considerations in the novel are many and are clearly underlined. The value of a novel as a work of art is, to some, dependent upon the lessons it teaches. The ideas Silas Marner touches are handled from a decidedly **didactic** viewpoint; the author, in her closings, often repeats the obvious interpretation suggested earlier.

Perhaps the most frequent adverse criticism of the novel is its excessive moralizing by the narrator. The explicit homilies, which many consider valuable for their teaching, are viewed by others as little more than superfluous sermonettes. In addition, certain of the scenes, such as Molly Farren trudging through the snow-covered lanes in the gloom or the renunciation of Godfrey by his child may appear, to today's readers, quaintly archaic or maudlin.

Question: What is the general plot structure of the novel?

Answer: There are two stories: one is of Silas Marner; the other is of Godfrey Cass. Their lives intersect three times. See A, B, and C.

Silas is born.

Silas is 24; he is found guilty of robbery at Lantern Yard.

Silas is 39 and has lived in Raveloe for fifteen years.

Godfrey is born.

Godfrey is 24; he marries Molly Farren; Eppie is born.

A. November: Theft of gold by Dunsey Cass.

B. December: Finding of Eppie in the snow. Molly Farren dies.

Silas rears Eppie.

Godfrey marries Nancy. He refuses to recognize Eppie as his child.

C. Silas is 55; Godfrey is 40. The body of Dunstan Cass is found. Godfrey tells Nancy of his marriage and child. Silas and Eppie refuse to part.

Wedding of Eppie.

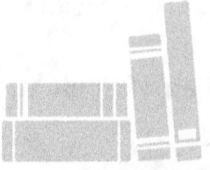

MIDDLEMARCH

PRELUDE

From rugged Avila, a Spanish town, St. Theresa ventured forth one day into the fearful land of the Moors. The innocent little girl and her younger brother had left to sow goodness and gain martyrdom-and both were stopped by their uncles.

Comment

One of the basic **themes** of *Middlemarch* is the disparity between one's idealistic goals and the difficulties which life provides to thwart them. St. Theresa and her brother represent idealism; their uncles symbolize reality.

It was an appropriate beginning for a child destined to become one of history's great women. The fuel that nourished the fire burning within her drove her to seek infinite satisfaction, the perfect good, a goal which could satisfy and justify a moral life, yet one of action as well as meditation. She attained her goal in the reform of a religious order.

Comment

There are many women born with spiritual grandeur similar to the Saint of Spain, but whose lives are unhistoric and uneventful on a grand scale. Their lives are filled with frustration, mistakes, and failure; their natures struggle against the barriers which society and circumstance impose. Because of the ardor they possess and the era and circumstances into which they are born, they are destined to be misunderstood, slandered, and ridiculed. Their ideals, although noble and well intentioned, are out of tune with the times and are considered eccentric. Such idealists are defeated by reality.

For the sake of clarity, George Eliot uses the brief prelude to state her **theme**: a universal conflict exists between individual growth and ambition in the face of adverse social or environmental conditions. Provincialism - of people devoted to material gratification and tolerant of culture only in its most superficial forms - is the barrier which our protagonists, Dorothea Brooke and Dr. Tertius Lydgate, must face. The intellectual and social desires of the inhabitants of Middlemarch have little sympathy or understanding for such idealists. Incapable of high aspirations themselves, Middlemarchers are inclined to allot petty or ignoble motives to those whom they cannot readily understand.

We are now about to be introduced to one of the finest panoramas of English provincial life in the early nineteenth century. It is a time of complex social, economic, and political change, which will leave England a more democratic country. It is, most particularly, a time of reform, an appropriate atmosphere for the rebellion of our characters against the general apathy of their society.

MIDDLEMARCH

TEXTUAL ANALYSIS

BOOK ONE: MISS BROOKE; CHAPTERS 1 - 12

....

CHAPTER ONE

The time is 1829: the place is Tipton Grange, a village in England. As the novel opens, we are introduced to the Brooke sisters, Dorothea and Celia. Dorothea, nineteen, and the older by a year, has that quality of beauty which "plain fashion seems to enhance." (The Virgin Mary and the Bible are both used in her description, giving us a clue as to her spiritual character.) She has "contagious charm" and enjoys riding and the outdoors, but her puritan conscience and her energy are at odds. Dorothea is naive, sympathetic, tender, magnanimous, and compulsive. Her sister Celia, on the other hand, is looked upon as the better prospect for marriage. She is amiable but practical, concerned more with outward appearances and impressions. She is, therefore, more "acceptable" by Middlemarch's provincial standards. Both are from an unquestionably "good" family, tracing back to the Puritans and Oliver Cromwell. Both their parents are dead; the girls are now staying at the country estate of their bachelor uncle, Mr. Arthur Brooke. He is a good-natured, foolish, and unpredictable gentleman of sixty-eight, whose grain of shrewdness makes him appealing and lovable. The sisters have inherited seven hundred pounds a year, and if Dorothea marries and has a son, he will inherit the Brooke estate. Dorothea, who is of a "theoretic" nature, yearns after "a lofty ideal," some principle which will justify her life and give meaning to her existence. The proper procedure for this quest, she believes, is to associate herself with some great man and assist him in bestowing his gifts for the benefit of mankind. She visualizes herself serving a man like John Milton or Thomas Hooker (profound English writers). Dorothea is entirely unaware of her attractiveness to the opposite sex and feels that all gentlemen visitors to the grange are in love with Celia. Dorothea's lofty ideals are looked upon by Middlemarch society as "peculiar," for conformity is the social and domestic temper of this society. Women are supposed to have weak opinions and passivity is given great value. Mr. Brooke is admonished continually by his social circle and by Mrs. Cadwallader, the rector's wife, in particular, for not having a middle-aged companion and guide for the girls.

The sisters are expecting two men for dinner that evening: Sir James Chettam, Dorothea's suitor, and Rev. Edward Causabon, a scholar of some reputation who is engaged in writing a long research work. During the day, Celia pleads with her sister to divide their mother's jewels, given to them by their uncle six months before. Dorothea is apathetic towards taking such worldly and superficial things but Celia energetically advances the following reasons for doing so.

Dorothea teases Celia, then relents, with a superior "Puritanic" tolerance. Celia has a placid nature that assents to her sister's sentiments but is never much disturbed by them. When viewing the jewels, Dorothea is reluctantly attracted to an emerald with diamonds (and in keeping with her spiritual nature compares it to the "spiritual emblems in the Revelation of St. John"). She keeps the emerald but suffers a pang of conscience when Celia intimates her inconsistency.

Comment

The first chapter of the novel introduces Dorothea Brooke to us. Clearly, she represents the idealistic and spiritual kind of woman whom Eliot describes in the Prelude. The differences between Dorothea and her sister Celia are noticed by the inhabitants of Middlemarch: to them Dorothea is an odd person because of her unusual values.

CHAPTER TWO

That evening at dinner, while Mr. Brooke discusses scientific farming and his acquaintances, Dorothea begins to form an impression of Reverend Casaubon. To her, he physically resembles the dignified and haunting portrait of John Locke, the English philosopher. She contrasts him with the vigorous Sir James Chettam. Mr. Brooke is opposed to the scientific approach to farming because it is too expensive and would lead to a complete reform. Dorothea argues that it would be to the good of the poor and the land. She idealistically states, "It is not a sin to make yourself poor in performing experiments for the good of all." Reverend Casaubon, who has been quietly observing, is impressed by Dorothea's energetic remark and fervor. After Mr. Brooke's generalizations on Adam Smith (an English economist) and Robert Southey (an English writer), Reverend Casaubon makes his first contribution to the conversation. We are informed that because of his research work on ancient times his eyes have been adversely affected, and so he must find someone to read for him. Reading has taken him much time, with the result that he has gotten "out of touch," so to speak: "I feed too much on the inward sources; I live too much with the dead."

Dorothea is much taken with Casaubon's learning and formality. She considers his attempt to reconstruct the past to be a very learned and noble venture. Here is the person she could associate herself with and help for the benefit of mankind. Mr. Brooke now discusses theology, Wilberforce (an English statesman and humanitarian) and the Catholic question (should Catholics be emancipated?), but Reverend Casaubon has been too busy with his studies to keep up on things. Brooke asks him how he keeps his documents organized. "In pigeon holes partly," replies Casaubon.

Comment

This reply gives us a suggestion of the narrowness and confinement of Casaubon.

Dorothea offers to organize her uncle's papers and Casaubon remarks that she would make a good "secretary."

Celia, discussing Casaubon in the drawing room, dislikes "the white moles" on his face; she also remarks that he is sallow; in general she considers him ugly and stuffy. Dorothea, or "Dodo" as Celia calls her sister, thinks he has a "great soul"; she reprimands Celia for judging a person by outward appearances only. Celia knows that Dorothea does not consider Sir James Chettam as a suitor, but he thinks she does. Much to her annoyance, Sir James continues to entreat Dorothea to give up horsemanship, until Casaubon intervenes by saying that Dorothea's motives must be respected and are no doubt of the highest merit. By forcing their revelation, they would tend to become less valuable. Sir James is forced to agree, but feels no jealousy since he believes Dorothea could not possibly be taken romantically with a "dried bookworm" of fifty like Casaubon. He then chats with Celia; when not near Dorothea, she talks freely. Sir James finds her amiable and pretty, although not superior to Dorothea.

CHAPTER THREE

The next morning, Dorothea continues her conversation with Reverend Casaubon, who is rector of Lowick (a town five miles from Tipton). He talks to her about the purpose of his work: to synthesize and find "A Key to All Mythologies" (the title of his work). To Dorothea, his ambitions and train of thought complement hers; subconsciously, she seeks a union with Casaubon. Because his research notes are voluminous he must condense them so that he can finally write and publish his work. The work, he reminds her, will take a great deal of time. Casaubon's explanation is delivered in a very scholarly and formal manner with very little emotion. Dorothea sees only what she wishes to see regarding Casaubon. She has faint stirrings that he can work to make her life "meaningful." She compares him to Jacques Bossuet (a French prelate, 1627-1704, author of Discourse on Universal History, 1681) and St. Augustine (the philosopher and theologian). Completely awed by his knowledge and understanding of the Ancients, she wishes to place her trust in him. Mr. Brooke persuades Casaubon to stay to view various documents and then to peruse his journal of travels. Casaubon politely tolerates him and is careful not to offend.

The next day Casaubon mentions to Dorothea that he has felt loneliness and the need of a youthful companion to lighten his "serious toils." This speech is made as if he were dictating a letter, it is so absent of feeling. After Casaubon leaves, Dorothea strolls in the woods, enjoying the autumnal loveliness. She contemplates her future with a man of such exalted purposes. She is very happy, although she realizes her idyllic love affair would be frowned upon by most young maidens of Middlemarch.

Comment

Because she is so ardent, intellectual, and theoretical, Dorothea romantically imagines herself a sharer in Casaubon's great goal: the completion of his book. She looks to Casaubon to lead her out of the narrow confines imposed upon her by society and the dismal passivity prescribed for women. He will "take her along the grandest path." She thinks his greatness will rub off on her.

She meets Sir James Chettam, whom she thinks is too patronizing. He remarks that he is envious of her power of forming an opinion, observing, "You seem to have the power of discrimination." He agrees to help Dorothea with her plans for building cottages for the workers on the estate. Perhaps she may be able to do the same at Lowick. Celia is sympathetic towards Sir James's illusion about Dorothea; she knows Dorothea is not impulsive and is amused at people who energetically express themselves.

Comment

Sir James' comment is ironic inasmuch as Dorothea's interest in Reverend Casaubon is hardly a "discriminating" one.

Casaubon now becomes a continual visitor, and Dorothea's first impressions of him are solidified. She likens his words to "a specimen from a mine, or the inscription on the door of a museum." She feels complimented when he appeals to her understanding or gives constructive criticism, but is disappointed when he shows lack of interest in her building plans. Mr. Brooke is invited to Lowick, and Dorothea and Sir James see each other often. She foresees a useful future for him with the right "feminine direction," and is most pleased that he is interested in her building plans.

> Comment

Witness how Casaubon's words suggest a mine and a museum. Dorothea sees both as classical references; we view them as dark, ancient, and lifeless places. Objectively, Casaubon lacks real human impulses and warmth but Dorothea's view of him clouds him in a romantic mist.

CHAPTER FOUR

Dorothea discovers from Celia that Sir James is in love with her and not her younger sister. This information is a product of gossip on the lower levels of Middlemarch society. Tantripp, Brooke's maid, heard it from Sir James's man, who knew it from Mrs. Cadwallader's maid. Dorothea realizes now that she has recognized signs of his love; her revulsion is so great that tears well up in her eyes. She feels she must discontinue her plans for the cottages with him, a plan which the villagers think is just a fad, another one of Dorothea's peculiarities. She is very upset to think that others consider her useful and noble motive for the buildings to be fanciful. Mr. Brooke returns and comments upon the fresh air during his drive home. (This description is in contrast to Lowick with its stale air and oppressive and tomblike atmosphere.) Mr. Brooke thinks Casaubon is too deep in books saying, he "mopes, you know." He has known Casaubon for ten years and has witnessed nothing productive from him. Because of Dorothea's age (nineteen), Casaubon has asked Brooke for her hand. She accepts him, much to the surprise of Brooke, who wishes her to marry Sir James. He tells Dorothea that Casaubon is not young and warns her that his health is weak, but he will not interfere. Dorothea's wish is to have a husband who is more profound than she, one who will show her "right opinions" and their ultimate value, so that she can build her life on them.

Mr. Brooke thinks he has presented the disadvantages of such a marriage to his niece; yet he recognizes that Casaubon's scholarly ways may suit her. Women are inconsistent anyway, and always a problem. He shrugs his shoulders, with the thought: "To judge what sort of marriage would turn out well for a young girl who prefers Casaubon to Chettam" is pure folly.

Comment

Dorothea's decision to marry Casaubon follows soon after her rejection of Sir Jame's offer of marriage. We see the pressure of a provincial social conscience brought to bear upon an altruistic person in the suffering Dorothea experiences when she learns of the townspeople's reaction to her building plans.

CHAPTER FIVE

The chapter opens with a letter which Reverend Casaubon has written as a marriage proposal to Dorothea. He gives an "accurate statement" of his feelings in inflated and pedantic prose. Casaubon describes Dorothea "as that rare combination of elements." He gives reasons for marriage: "To supply aid in graver labors and to cast a charm over vacant hours." Dorothea is overwhelmed and grateful; now she will be able to grow intellectually and morally; she need no longer repress her ardent nature. She answers him immediately, seeing no reason to delay her reply. Dorothea frets about her penmanship, hoping to make a good impression on Casaubon. In her reply she expresses her utmost gratitude for the proposal and happily anticipates their marriage. Her uncle advises her to be cautious, giving a last plea for Sir James, but she is adamant. Brooke acquiesces with a speech on how scholarly pursuits interested him at one time. He knows also that Mrs. Cadwallader will have much to say to him.

Comment

Notice how conscious of social criticism the people of Middlemarch are.

That evening, Celia supposes that Dorothea's agitated condition is caused by the disappointment over Sir James and the building plans. Before retiring, Dorothea tells Celia she is very happy; Celia thinks it is strange to go from one extreme to another. Casaubon is invited to dinner and Celia senses Dorothea's excitement when he accepts her invitation. Celia becomes a little alarmed when the thought crosses her mind that Casaubon might mean something serious to "Dodo." Dorothea (in a pensive mood now) is debating whether to tell Celia of their engagement. Celia begins to ridicule Reverend Casaubon's foibles: he scrapes his spoon in his soup bowl and blinks before he speaks. It is then that Dorothea tells Celia of her engagement.

Celia is shocked, but tenderness surmounts other feelings and she apologizes, wishing her sister happiness.

Dorothea still believes that Tipton criticizes her marriage. Upon seeing Casaubon later that evening, she pledges herself to him and he is flattered. She begs him to show her how she may best serve him to further all his great ends. Casaubon considers her "ardent self-sacrificing affection" to be an admirable quality. His frigid rhetoric is supplied with warmth and sincerity by Dorothea's sympathetic but limited point of view. They find themselves happy together and decide to marry within six weeks.

Comment

Dorothea has now practically sealed her avenues of escape. Her "theoretical" nature is composed both of genuine innocence of the ways of the world and of a kind of moral shortsightedness which mistakes prison for liberty.

CHAPTER SIX

Mrs. Cadwallader, wife of the rector of Tipton and Freshitt, passes Casaubon on her way to visit Mr. Brooke. She stops to gossip and bargain with the lodgekeeper about poultry. Mrs. Cadwallader is of "immeasurably" high birth and known to the farmers and laborers of that area as an inquisitive, witty, and sharp woman who "pleaded" poverty, and "pared down" prices. However, if anyone were to get too familiar, she would remind them of who she was. She often chides Brooke about entertaining Casaubon and threatens to expose him as a Whig and a Catholic Bill sympathizer; she also warns him against running for office as an independent. Known as a "matchmaker," she is very surprised when Brooke tells her that Dorothea will not marry Sir James, who is Mrs. Cadwallader's choice. When questioned as to whom she will marry, Mr. Brooke makes a hasty exit, to avoid the sharp tongue of the rector's wife. He leaves this unpleasant task to Celia. Mrs. Cadwallader thinks the whole affair is "frightful" but knows it had to be Dorothea's idea. She will now devote her talents to uniting Celia and Sir James. When she informs Sir James of the impending marriage, he expresses disgust and compares Casaubon to a mummy. They know Brooke will never be talked into disapproving the match. Before Mrs. Cadwallader leaves, she advises Sir James that Celia is impressed with him. He resolves to ride to Tipton Grange because he wants to meet the challenge of being a "good sport" about the intended marriage and because he knows Celia will be there, a thought which makes him feel better about the situation.

Comment

Mrs. Cadwallader is a familiar figure in literature: the solicitous matron whose chief vocation is to determine which unsuspecting men and women she can manage to manipulate into marriage. Such flabby cupids, soaring with arrows poised, shall, like lovers, always be with us.

CHAPTER SEVEN

In the time prior to the marriage, Reverend Casaubon visits the Grange often. He has deliberately put aside his research to relax and enjoy Dorothea's companionship. He finds his stream of desire quite shallow and thinks the poets exaggerate the "force of masculine passion." He cannot find the cause of his lack of ardor in any deficiency of Dorothea. She expresses a wish to learn Latin and Greek so that she may be of greater assistance to him and to develop her range of knowledge. She has a selfish motive also because she feels this "realm of masculine scholarship" may hold the "core of things": armed with learning she may be able to interpret correctly the social duties of a Christian. Casaubon consents reluctantly to instruct Dorothea. He finds it disagreeable and is unable to answer her questions intelligently, but it is Dorothea who feels that she lacks the intellectual depth for such an endeavor. Mr. Brooke, of course, agrees with her. He feels such profound studies as the classics and mathematics are too taxing for any woman. Dorothea would be "better employed" studying music. (She knows little about that art because at this time it was discouraged.) Casaubon can only tolerate with moderation "grander forms of music worthy to accompany solemn celebrations." He can accept only those forms approved by ancient conception. Mr. Brooke regards Dorothea's hopes as "unhealthy" and instructs Casaubon to have a quieting influence on his niece. He thinks Casaubon is affluent, and a sensible person; perhaps someday he may even become a dean or a bishop.

Comment

Observe how Eliot gradually cracks the plaster of the saint Dorothea imagines Casaubon to be.

CHAPTER EIGHT

In this chapter, we are concerned primarily with Sir James's attempts to prevent the match. He finds it easier now to visit the Grange after his initial encounter with Dorothea. He feels no jealousy toward Casaubon, but is shocked that Dorothea labors under this "melancholy illusion." Sir James, convinced that Mr. Brooke should have prevented the match, visits rector Cadwallader (who is a good friend), and asks him to intervene on the grounds that Dorothea is not of age. At first, the rector thinks that Sir James wants him to stop Brooke from running for office on the Whig ticket. (The rector's remark is indicative of the general feeling towards Brooke's political aspirations.) Anyone who is anti-Whig should be very happy when the Whigs fail to select the strongest candidate to run. He soon realizes that the visit is not for this purpose. Sir James tells the rector that both he and Celia have judged Casaubon alike; he remarks, "He is fifty and he never could have been much of a man." When the rector asks the reasons for Chettam's dislike, Sir James is stunned to think that the rector is not in sympathy with him. He asks, "Has he got any heart?" The rector proceeds to tell of Casaubon's fair and just treatment of his relatives. Sir James is still unconvinced, informing Cadwallader that his motive for trying to stop the marriage is simply because he believes that Dorothea will suffer for it.

Mrs. Cadwallader enters with her young son; she tells Sir James that she and her husband have "washed their hands" of the affair. One last plea is made by Sir James but it is repulsed by the rector. He feels that Casaubon has done his duty to his profession, has done no visible harm to anyone and, finally, that he apparently loves Dorothea.

Afterwards, Sir James, maintaining his good disposition, continues to help Dorothea with her cottages, enjoying her company even more now that there is no "passion to hide or confess."

CHAPTER NINE

Dorothea wishes to see her new home at Lowick to make any changes necessary.

Comment

George Eliot's humorous maxim is appropriate here: "A woman dictates before marriage in order that she may have an appetite for submission afterwards."

Dorothea travels to Lowick with her uncle and Celia, who does not fail to point out the depressing aspects of the manor house at Lowick. It is an old-fashioned house; on this gray November morning the southern and eastern parts of the house appear "rather melancholy": the grounds are more confining and the flower beds need tending. The manor is small-windowed and has an air of "autumnal decline." It is a home which needs flowers, children, and open windows to make it livable. Dorothea sees great possibilities and imagines the house to be "hallowed."

Comment

To Dorothea, the dark bookshelves and faded curtains and carpets have been subdued by time. An old vase here and there and curious old maps and other images help to suggest how depressing Reverend Casaubon is, for the house is a reflection of his personality.

Dorothea sees no changes to be made. Casaubon inquires as to which room she would prefer. She has no favorite but

Celia does, and Mr. Brooke comments that the bow-windowed room would be nice after some alterations. Dorothea wants no changes. Mr. Casaubon points out his aunt among a group of miniatures in the room, but tells Dorothea little about her other than that she had an unfortunate marriage. Celia, in an aside, tells her sister that she recently saw a young man (Will Ladislaw), who physically resembled Casaubon's aunt. They then meet Mr. Tucker, the curate (a minor clergyman). He is unfavorable in Celia's eyes because the "corners of his mouth are so unpleasant." She dreads the time she must spent as bridesmaid at Lowick. Mr. Tucker answers Dorothea's questions, but she is disappointed that the people of the village appear well and satisfied, because now there is nothing she can do for them. She then makes a mental note to devote more time to Casaubon's aims.

In the garden of the manor house, Dorothea meets the young man whom Celia had mentioned as resembling Casaubon's aunt. He is Will Ladislaw, Casaubon's second cousin and the grandson of his Aunt Julia. She looks at the sketches he is drawing and makes an innocent comment which he misunderstands as criticism. Ladislaw thinks Dorothea must be unpleasant and certainly can have no passion if she is to marry Casaubon. We learn from Casaubon that Ladislaw attended Rugby but refused to go to an English university. It was his choice to study at Heidelberg. He now wants to go abroad for "cultural preparation."

Comment

From this first impression we may considered Will Ladislaw to be unsettled; Eliot depicts him as a "dabbler" in the arts, reformer, and a freethinker.

Casaubon is supporting Will and is paying for his education. He has tried to give Will a sense of responsibility and discipline, feeling they are necessary prerequisites for a life's vocation. He underscores that his own manuscript is the result of hard work, discipline, and preparation for a work not yet accomplished. Dorothea thinks Casaubon to be very noble for having patience with young Ladislaw by continuing to support and guide him.

Comment

One suspects that Will has a better understanding of Casaubon than Casaubon has of him.

CHAPTER TEN

Will decides not to fix his European destination any more precisely than the "Continent." He feels that genius must not be confined but must have the opportunity to receive its motivation from a wide number of stimuli. He has drunk wine excessively and has experimented with opium to see what effects they would have on his creativity. Nothing original resulted from these measures. He thinks it is only a matter of time before his genius will evolve. He feels Casaubon's impotence with his work to be no example to follow.

Comment

Eliot now shifts her attention to Casaubon. She makes a plea for tolerance for him, suggesting that anyone would have come in for their share of criticism from Mrs. Cadwallader, Mr. Brooke,

Sir James, and Celia. Certainly, in spite of Casaubon's rigid method of discourse and his unimpassioned nature, we should not imagine he has no feeling or good work in him at all.

Naturally enough, Casaubon considers himself to be the center of his universe. He is touched by thoughts of his forthcoming marriage, but is surprised to find that his spirit is not rising; he is disappointed because he is not more enchanted by romance. Inasmuch as he had restrained his emotions and rationed his affection, he thought he would now have an abundance to use. He finds he is more barren of sensibilities at the very time they should be most ripe. Utterly alone and despairing, he fears he is endlessly toiling-sifting his mass of notes-yet getting no closer to his goal.

Dorothea, on the other hand, is looking forward to marriage with great expectations. It will open new vistas of learning for her. It is decided that Rome is to be the destination of the wedding trip. Casaubon suggests a traveling companion for Dorothea since he will be very busy doing research in culturally rich Rome. Dorothea is hurt, not so much because Casaubon may neglect her on their honeymoon, but because he shuns her help in his research.

There is a party at the Grange, the last preliminary preparation for the wedding. Dorothea is the subject of many observations this evening. Some of the guests include the newly elected mayor of Middlemarch (Mr. Vincy), who "happened to be a manufacturer," and his brother-in-law the philanthropic banker, Mr. Bulstrode, who is called by different names by the townspeople ("hypocrite," "Methodist dissenter"). Before reform took hold there was a clearer distinction of class in Middlemarch, and this party was considered too "miscellaneous" for many of the people. The variety of guests is the product of Mr. Brooke's liberal leanings and "inordinate travel." At the party, several of the men discuss their preferences in women. Mr. Chichely, a middle-aged bachelor, indicates his preference for flirtatious, coquettish women. He holds up the mayor's daughter. Rosamond Vincy, as an example of an ideal woman. The women at the party make fun of Casaubon's "drying up of passion"; they judge Dorothea to be excessively "earnest." We are introduced to Dr. Lydgate in the women's conversation. They describe him to be clever and a gentleman with a "fine brow."

Comment

Dr. Lydgate, one of the novel's major figures, is indeed a gentleman. He comes from a good background, which was quite unusual for medical men at that time. The profession was mistrusted, misunderstood, and was considered to be one of the lesser vocations for gentlemen.

Lydgate is reputed to be treating fever in a way different from the usual manner. He makes a good impression on Lady Chettam because he neither agrees or disagrees with her. A very clever conversationalist, he never offends. He has studied in Paris, where he met outstanding men, and he has ideas for raising the standards of the medical profession. Lydgate is unimpressed when he meets Dorothea.

Soon after the party, the marriage takes place and the Reverend and Mrs. Casaubon leave for Rome on their wedding trip.

Comment

Witness how Eliot captures the life of Middlemarch by presenting social situations. In this instance, she shows us a prewedding party, complete with its gallery of character types and gossip.

At this point in the novel the attention will shift from Dorothea Brooke to Dr. Lydgate. Eliot introduces us to him in this transitional chapter because succeeding chapters will be concerned with his fortunes. A second plot, then, is about to begin.

CHAPTER ELEVEN

Dr. Lydgate is very much attracted to a young girl noticeably different from Dorothea Brooke: Rosamond Vincy. Anxious to start his medical practice, he feels that love and marriage are impractical until he becomes firmly established in his profession. To Lydgate. Dorothea is too inquisitive, opinionated, and moralistic.

Comment

Lydgate's error here it that he is unable to see deeper into a person's character.

His ambition is to reform the medical professional of his time, and such a hope is not conducive to getting rich quickly. Wealth, however, is secondary to Lydgate. Rosamond was the pride of Mrs. Lemon's school, a sort of finishing school for girls who sought to acquire the social graces. Lydgate is attracted by the superficial characteristics of Rosamond. The Vincy family is socially prominent: Mr. Vincy's sister Harriet married the wealthy, influential banker, Nicholas Bulstrode, who as considered to have improved himself by this marriage. Mr. Vincy married an innkeeper's daughter and Mrs. Vincy's sister was the second wife to rich old Mr. Featherstone, but she had died childless years ago. Lydgate inherits Mr. Featherstone and Bulstrode as patients. Rosamond wishes her father would employ Dr. Lydgate since she is bored with the local young men; stranger would be an exciting diversion. She has no patience with her brothers, especially Fred, whose father in anxious for him to take a degree and become a minister. Fred is opposed to such future and spends his time in the pursuit of pleasure, much to the consternation of his good-natured mother. Rosamond and Fred tease each other constantly. She considers it a disadvantage to have been born a daughter of a Middlemarch manufacturer and is ashamed that her mother was the daughter of an innkeeper. Her mother wanted Rosamond to go to Featherstone's home "Stone Court" when Mrs. Vincy's sister died, but she refused. A girl named Mary Garth now attends to Mr. Featherstone's needs, and there is a fear that she will inherit some of his money. Fred informs Rosamond that their uncle is ill and that he is going to visit him, when Dr. Lydgate goes to attend him. Rosamond looks upon the visit as an opportunity to meet the new doctor; she decides to go along with Fred.

CHAPTER TWELVE

The wealthy Peter Featherstone is very seriously ill and is visited by his sister, Mrs. Waule, at Stone Court in Lowick parish. Wealthy in her own rights, she has fear of anyone other than the Featherstones inheriting her brother's money, and suggests to him how unsteady his favorite nephew Fred is, with his constant gambling at billiards. She asserts that he has borrowed a good deal of money on the strength of his inheritance when Featherstone dies, a fact she has learned from her brother Solomon. She attempts to gain Featherstone's favor for his nephew John on the Featherstone side of the family. Mrs. Waule is afraid that Mary Garth will side with Fred in order to gain Featherstone's favor but Mary tells her she is not interested in any scandal. When Fred and Rosamond arrive, Peter speaks alone to his nephew, informing him of what he has just heard from his sister. Fred denies the rumor (for he really had never borrowed in this way). Featherstone mischievously hints that Bulstrode was the informer and wishes Fred to solicit a letter from Bulstrode stating that the banker has good faith in Fred's honor not to borrow money on the security of his (Featherstone's) land. This letter, Peter observes, will vindicate Fred. Fred has a problem, for he knows that Bulstrode, like other men, believes in rumors and that Bulstrode dislikes him. Fred appeals to his uncle's vanity by saying that the whole procedure is not gentlemanly. Peter has little use for Bulstrode, viewing him as a religious hypocrite, who is always fortifying his questionable dealings with a religious motive or justification. Good, solid land is God-given, but "speculating" is inspired by the devil, exclaims Peter. Peter promises to back Fred's debts "a bit" if the letter is delivered.

Rosamond and Mary, who had been lifelong acquaintances and attended the same provincial school, were enjoying their conversation. Mary, compared to Rosamond, appears very plain but has no illusions about life or herself. Shrewd and a little satirical, she is strong-willed and has a sense of obligation to her family. Mary is very receptive to sincerity but will not extend herself to those who "speak to me, without seeming to see me." She is in sympathy with Fred's rejection of the ministry but censors his aimlessness and idle ways. Rosamond's opinions appear superficial and vacant when compared with Mary's.

Some of Rosamond's ideas about topics discussed during their brief chat are: (1) Love: interesting and agreeable people fall in love when in close proximity for any length of time. (2) Religion: it is a crutch to lean on when there are no other prospects in view. (3) Vocation: the vocation makes the man. Mary finds that Fred is in love with her but she will not marry him until he has matured and proven himself in some worthy vocation.

Dr. Lydgate arrives, a little disillusioned with Middlemarch charm and the prospect of his visit with Featherstone. Rosamond consciously dramatizes all her actions for the sole purpose of attracting Lydgate's favor. She succeeds admirably and when their eyes meet as he gives Rosamond her riding whip, she feels they have fallen in love! It had to happen this way, Rosamond contemplates, because she had constructed her future this way. On her way home she has reveries that Lydgate is in love with her; her brother Fred is meditating on his visit with his uncle; he knows that Featherstone enjoys tormenting him but does not realize that Peter had been teasing him about Bulstrode's informing him (Featherstone) of his debts. He hopes that his father will take upon himself the unpleasant task of speaking to Bulstrode.

MIDDLEMARCH

TEXTUAL ANALYSIS

BOOK TWO: OLD AND YOUNG; CHAPTERS 13 - 22

CHAPTER THIRTEEN

Mr. Bulstrode, the banker, is visited by Dr. Lydgate. Bulstrode wishes him to become superintendent of the new hospital which he is building in Middlemarch. Some men distrust Bulstrode because of his looks, his verbose speech, and his scrutiny of others in conversation. The villagers of Middlemarch are suspicious of his little-known past. Dr. Lydgate suggests a special wing for treatment of contagious diseases and has high hopes, after his reforms have taken hold, of starting a medical school. All his ideas are put forth in a confident manner and with a convincing mode of delivery. He has little regard for the obstacles to his ideas, but his good will saves him from being overbearing. Particularly impressed by the doctor because he is a stranger, Bulstrode cautions Lydgate about the possible jealousy of his fellow practitioners when they learn of his appointment as superintendent. Lydgate replies that he enjoys a good fight. Bulstrode now alludes to the spiritual condition of patients. He shows his political sense by suggesting that the doctor support Mr. Tyke over Mr. Farebrother for the paid position of chaplain at the hospital, although the proposed building stands in Mr. Farebrother's parish and he has been attending patients of the old hospital without compensation. Lydgate defers his judgment because a decision of this sort lies outside the realm of medical knowledge. Bulstrode then intimates that he has an ulterior financial motive for his interest in the affairs of the hospital. As Lydgate is leaving he meets and accepts a dinner invitation from Mr. Vincy, who has come in behalf of his son Fred. Mr. Bulstrode is quick to point out the errors of others and reprimands Vincy for his son's behavior; he suggests that it was not a spiritual motive but rather a worldly one which prompted Vincy to encourage his son to enter the clerical life. Vincy resents Bulstrode's superior attitude, especially in light of the prospect of his (Vincy's) becoming mayor, but he **refrains** from being argumentative. Mr. Vincy finally explains the purpose of his visit. Bulstrode suggests that he would not be surprised if the rumor of Fred's borrowing on the prospect of his uncle's death is true. Mr. Vincy argues that Fred would not lie to him or to anyone. Bulstrode thinks that by vindicating Fred and paving the way for his inheritance he will be doing Fred an injustice. "I cannot regard wealth as a blessing to those who use it simply as a harvest for this world." Vincy desperately attacks Bulstrode by suggesting that he is dishonest in one of his business partnerships: "Plymdale's house uses those blue and green dyes it gets from the Brassing manufactory; they rot the silk. . . ." Bulstrode assumes Vincy is taking advantage of his relationship as his brother-in-law. Vincy angrily tells Bulstrode that families should stick together and help one another; he warns Bulstrode that if he does not write the letter he (Vincy) will consider it "unhandsome and will not bear it well." He views a failure to support Fred's honor to be in fact spreading scandal about Fred. Bulstrode promises to consult his wife before making a decision.

> Comment

Bulstrode represents the author's view of a religious hypocrite, one who is most careful to maintain a spiritual exterior for business purposes, yet is quick to bend his ethical principles if personal gain may ensue.

CHAPTER FOURTEEN

The next day, Bulstrode writes the letter; Fred brings it to Peter Featherstone. It is very cleverly worded to absolve Fred of the rumor, yet it avoids any direct statements denying Fred's action. Old Featherstone is very disagreeable to Mary Garth since he has become ill. He enjoys taunting Fred about the monetary gift he is about to offer him. Much to Fred's disappointment the money he is given totals one hundred pounds, sixty less than his debt. Fred covers his disappointment and, when finally dismissed, seeks Mary.

In the conversation that ensues, we see the strong bond of the Garth family. Mary displays remarkable good judgment and common sense despite her strong feeling for Fred. Fred alludes to John Waule's love for her. Mary answers, "I have no ground for the nonsensical vanity of fancying everybody who comes near me is in love with me. I think any hardship is better than pretending to do what one is paid for, and never really doing it." Mary, goodnaturedly yet without any possibility of Fred's misunderstanding her meaning, reprimands him for his irresponsibility and debts. However, Fred is still very much impressed with the "higher education of the country," an impression which has distorted his respect of income and rank. He tries to get Mary to declare her love for him by saying a man can do nothing worthwhile unless he has the love of a woman. Mary thinks it would be an injustice to marry a man who is idle, although she might love him. Anyway, her father would not accept a shiftless man. She encourages him to pass his examinations but will promise him nothing. She cautions Fred never to speak to her of marriage and love again until he is gainfully employed. Fred is chagrined because it is Mary's father who is the signer of the bill which Fred owes to his creditor.

CHAPTER FIFTEEN

This chapter gives us background material about Dr. Lydgate and how he became interested in medicine. After attending public school he was orphaned and left in the care of guardians. He discovered an anatomy book by accident in his home library and soon dedicated himself to the study of medicine. He studied in London, Edinburgh, and Paris. In his youth, Lydgate was emotional. warm-hearted, and rash. He had a peculiar resistance to serious study, but was interested in human beings; he was a man as well as a doctor. He became attracted by the need for reform in the medical profession and judged the best opportunity for it and for serious medical work would be away from the city, in a provincial town where he could "win celebrity." Interested only in prescribing drugs (not dispensing them) and doing original work, Lydgate was fired with an ideal to become a perfect, dedicated doctor. He was ambitious to enlarge the scientific basis of his profession. At twenty-seven, Lydgate had become involved with an actress in Paris and offered to marry her through "impetuous folly" after she had been accused of killing her husband. To his sorrow, Lydgate discovered that she had meant to kill him out of hate; it was not chance, as he had believed. Disillusioned with women and determined to remain aloof, he had decided to settle down to a life of service and research in Middlemarch.

CHAPTER SIXTEEN

The question of appointing Mr. Tyke as hospital chaplain is an interesting topic to the people of Middlemarch. It indicates the power of the banker Mr. Bulstrode; he knows the financial secrets of most of the businessmen of the town since he administers the town charities. There are those who are openly opposed to him, and those who are openly opposed to him, and those who go the way the wind blows. Bulstrode willingly confers obligations, but is "severe" in watching the results. The more power he wins the better he learns to use it for the "glory of God." His "spiritual conflict" consists of adjusting his motives to harmonize with God's glory.

Mr. Vincy tells his dinner guest, Dr. Lydgate, that he favors Mr. Farebrother, who is a likeable person and who gives human and reasonable sermons, but he is opposed to Tyke because of his dogmatism (inflexible religious beliefs). Mr. Chichely, the coroner, wishes to have the directors and medical board decide the issue. Dr. Sprague (who has not kept up on medical changes) frowns upon the "foreign ideas" of Lydgate, who chooses to be outspoken and rash deliberately to encourage the disfavor of men like Chichely and Sprague.

At dinner, Lydgate and Rosamond become engrossed in conversation. She appears even more refined when compared to the unpretentiousness and "inoffensive vulgarity" of Mrs. Vincy.

Rosamond is perfectly attuned to the social graces but lacks humor. She is an excellent singer and Lydgate is charmed. In short, he finds her utterly attractive and accomplished. Mr. Farebrother enters and soon extends an invitation to Lydgate to dine with him. He then proceeds to play a serious game of whist. Lydgate watches the game until eleven, when he leaves. He finds himself liking Farebrother, whose church is the oldest in Middlemarch and whose salary is barely enough to meet his needs. He next meditates on Rosamond, judging that when he is ready to marry in a few years he would like his wife to be like her: a girl who possesses intelligence, grace, and talents. Lydgate thinks that he is not likely to make the same mistake with Miss Vincy as he did with the Parisian actress. After all, he only "admires" Rosamond. At home, he decides to look into Louis' view on fever. Dr. Lydgate is happy in his work, not only for its intellectual content, but because of its involvement with human beings.

We leave his higher plane of thought to descend, somewhat, to Rosamond. She is not concerned with the state of mankind or with any occupation, but rather with a coquettish "inward repetition of looks, words and phrases." Rosamond sees no reason to delay her marriage plans, since she never questions whether Lydgate is in love with her. She vainly assumes that all men fall in love with her sooner or later. In her mind he is what she always dreamed of. He has all the necessary characteristics for her story-book romance.

Comment

The parallel between the budding love of Rosamond and Dr. Lydgate and the love of Dorothea and Casaubon is obvious. Both men view marriage somewhat reluctantly; the women view it romantically.

CHAPTER SEVENTEEN

Lydgate is invited to dine at the home of Mr. Farebrother. The house is old and dated. He lives with his mother, his aunt (Miss Noble), and Miss Winifred Farebrother, his older sister. His mother "was evidently accustomed to tell her company what they ought to think, and to regard no subject as quite safe without her steering." She informs Lydgate that they are not often in want of medical aid, since she is very careful in rearing her children.

Farebrother tells Lydgate that his ideals will not be easy to forward since the conservative Middlemarch society will fight him to preserve the status quo. Farebrother gives Lydgate good advice. With acute insight into human motives and acts, he tells him to keep himself independent of others, perfect his knowledge so people will realize his value, and choose a good wife-an unworldly woman. (He gives Miss Garth as a perfect example.)

Mr. Farebrother shows Dr. Lydgate his collection of nature-study specimens. Lydgate senses that this man of the cloth may have desired a different vocation. (Perhaps the dominance of his mother was responsible for his choice of the ministry over nature study.) Farebrother, who changes the topic from nature study, suggests that Lydgate avail himself of Bulstrode's favor and assistance by voting for Mr. Tyke as chaplain. He confides to Lydgate that they should remain friends, regardless of how he votes.

CHAPTER EIGHTEEN

Lydgate, who really has little interest in the question of the chaplaincy and who would have voted for Mr. Tyke out of convenience, is hesitant now because of his developing friendship with Mr. Farebrother. Lydgate admires his sacrificing of his own interest for his mother, sister, and aunt; furthermore, his generosity and delicacy for Lydgate's situation a e exemplary. Mr. Farebrother's character and conduct are unusually fine, and his sermons (delivered without a book), are attended by people outside his parish.

At Mr. Bulstrode's request, Dr. Lydgate is laying plans for the interior of the hospital. The voting has been given to the board of directors and the medical men; Lydgate knows he has to decide how to vote.

Comment

We see Lydgate faced with a possible loss of his independence if he succumbs to outside pressures; he realizes a vote for Tyke ensures an office for him, while a vote for Farebrother will result in the loss of the office.

Now Lydgate begins to rationalize his position and looks for faults in Farebrother: (1) He spends too much time on non-clerical occupations. (2) He plays cards for money. (3) He plays billiards frequently at the Green Dragon. (4) He probably does not care for the job but is more interested in the money. However, Lydgate thinks he can vote for Farebrother if there is no valid objection to him from anyone else, since he fears a vote for Tyke will make him a vassal of Bulstrode's. During the voting, Bulstrode becomes identified with Lydgate, and Lydgate with Tyke because of gossip begun by the doctors and the directors. Lydgate is not popular with medical men because of his ideas on reform; in addition, they take it as an insult to their standing because he has refused to "dispense" drugs.

Bulstrode's enemies become Lydgate's, because of their alleged friendship. The vote ends in a draw and Lydgate, when angered by the remark of a Mr. Wrench that he is sure to vote the way Bulstrode does, rashly does vote that way, the chaplaincy is given to Mr. Tyke. Lydgate's conscience is troubled about this for some time after.

Comment

The integrity of Lydgate is swayed by the pettiness of the Middlemarch doctors and his own emotion. One of the major **themes** in the novel is the conflict between idealists and the obstacles which reality places in their paths.

CHAPTER NINETEEN

In this chapter we return to the story of Dorothea and her husband, Rev. Casaubon. Will Ladislaw, traveling in Rome, learns from a German artist (Adolf Naumann), of a woman of artistic beauty he has seen in the museum, and whom he wants Will to see. Much to Will's surprise, he discovers the woman is Dorothea. Adolf wishes to know if she is really married, since he has mistaken Casaubon for her father! Will tells him that Casaubon is, indeed, her husband and that she is also his cousin. Naumann wishes to paint her and expresses his desire to Will, who becomes very much disturbed about the idea and at first refuses. Naumann suggests the possibility of jealousy, which Ladislaw rejects openly. Yet Will does have certain misgivings about his motives; why did he object so strenuously to his friend's proposed portrait of Dorothea?

Comment

Eliot's interest in the psychological aspects of a character is shown in the introspection Ladislaw undergoes concerning his possible jealousy.

CHAPTER TWENTY

We find Dorothea in her apartment in the Via Sistina, sobbing bitterly. She has been in Rome five weeks and her puritanic conceptions are blinding her to the city's treasures. She is content only when she can be close to earth and sky-away from the "oppressive masquerade" of the ages. Casaubon spends little time with his melancholic bride. Her ardent nature, combined with English and Swiss puritanism make her view the culture of Rome in the light of irreverence and decay. She is thoroughly upset and lonely. To see the sensual and spiritual motifs of the Renaissance intermingled confuses her and checks her flow of responsive emotion.

Comment

Casaubon, not Rome, is the cause of Dorothea's depression. Eliot uses Rome to suggest the disappointment Dorothea finds in her new husband.

Dorothea's view of her marriage is now beginning to change slightly although she is not aware of it. Casaubon only confuses her whenever she wishes to learn or to improve her understanding. She senses that she will never be able to aid him in his work. Casaubon lacks interest or sympathy in the face of the art and other great treasures of Rome; he seems fearful of committing himself to opinions, lest his superficial knowledge be discovered.

Comment

Like Lydgate, Dorothea is warm and affectionate; had Casaubon at least responded accordingly she would have been content. Without response, however, her suffering is acute.

Because of the turmoil inside her, Dorothea is disagreeable to Casaubon when he informs her that his study is not quite finished; although he has kept her away from Rome during the holidays he hopes that she is enjoying herself in his absence. He compliments her by saying that she has lightened his burden of thought when he is not studying. This remark is delivered with an absence of emotion or feeling, characteristic of his stylistically frigid, pedantic language. For the first time Dorothea asks him to make up his mind which notes of research he will use, and to begin to write the book and publish it. She pleads that she will do anything to help him attain this end. Her idea strikes a note of fear in Casaubon, because Dorothea may discover his lack of confidence in his ability to actually write the work. He becomes suspicious of her and is hurt by her perception of his pretenses to scholarship. Casaubon covers his stress by stating that he is an authority and knows when the book should be written; he tells Dorothea that she is incompetent to judge such a grand and profound undertaking. Dorothea then asks him why he never speaks of writing the work, instead of always discussing his row of notebooks!

To Dorothea's "ardent" nature, this first disagreement seems a **catastrophe**. To Casaubon, who already has been disappointed because of his lack of feeling during their marriage, Dorothea's plan is a new "pain"; he suffers in the knowledge that she is capable of hurting him cruelly. The couple drive to the Vatican in silence; when he departs, Naumann first glimpses her beside the statue. (Eliot uses the flashback technique here.)

Comment

Dorothea is now aware that her new husband is less of a warm, responsive person and more of a cold, disciplined note-taker than she had imagined.

CHAPTER TWENTY-ONE

Hurriedly drying her tears, Dorothea opens the door of the apartment to a visitor, Will Ladislaw. Aware of her husband's generosity toward Will, she hopes that she may now help her husband in his kind deeds. Casaubon is away for the whole day at the Vatican Library, feverishly filling his notebooks, for the Casaubons are soon to leave Rome. Privately, Will is annoyed with his cousin for leaving his new bride at home, alone, while he pursues his insignificant details elsewhere. Dorothea speaks of her confusion and negative feelings when viewing so many art treasures in Rome. In her simplicity, she tells Will to become an artist and to improve upon the great paintings of Rome; when he shows apathy towards such a vocation she chides him, like Casaubon does, for his lack of patience. Will states, "He and I differ." Dorothea, although she has just been reminiscing about her husband's tutorial manner and lack of warmth, speaks glowingly about his devotion to study. Such comments annoy Will, for he fails to understand how Dorothea can be so deceived by Casaubon. Much to her consternation, Will suggests that Casaubon's labors may be unnecessary because of the strides in research now being made by German historians. After his retort Will is contrite, because he feels he has hurt Dorothea's feelings.

He is very much impressed by her simplicity, generous feeling, and good nature and has a strong desire to help her understand Casaubon's false pretenses. Dorothea feels very responsive to Will and thanks him, thinking he understands her. She needs Will to talk to, to fill her lonely hours.

Casaubon enters and proceeds to exhibit all his usual dullness and formality. Even though he is unpleasantly surprised to find Will there, he never gives such an impression, remaining his imperturbable self. He invites Will to dinner the following evening. After Will leaves, Casaubon receives an apology from Dorothea for her disagreeable behavior at breakfast. Casaubon accepts it without much feeling and is tempted (by jealousy) to expose his dislike of meeting Will. Dorothea is now aware of her "wild illusion" of expecting a response from her husband; also, she discerns that there is a weakness in his character, which is in need of understanding on her part.

Comment

We witness Dorothea's attempts to adjust to her marriage. Although she is becoming aware of Casaubon's faults, Dorothea considers herself obliged to consider his feelings also.

CHAPTER TWENTY-TWO

Next evening at dinner, all is pleasant: the displeasure the Reverend Casaubon has experienced from his cousin's presence has been mollified and Will is ingratiatingly agreeable company. Dorothea and her husband even accept an invitation to accompany Will on a tour of artists' studios on the following day. Inevitably, they end their tour at Adolf Neumann's studio. Naumann is busily painting when they enter. His interest at present lies in spiritual and religious subjects, and he asks Casaubon to pose for the head of St. Thomas Aquinas. Casaubon is obviously flattered and allows Dorothea to pose for Santa Clara while he rests. He agrees to return the following day. Dorothea begins to feel differently about Rome and its treasures: she begins to feel exhilarated. Will is annoyed with Adolf when he rhapsodizes on Dorothea's beauty.

Will wants desperately to leave a lasting impression on Dorothea. He decides to visit her alone, without an invitation. Unaware of her husband's feeling about Will, Dorothea welcomes him enthusiastically, for she enjoys his company and thinks they complement one another. She expresses to Will her desire to make life beautiful for all and her sorrow at the thought of anyone's being deprived of a decent life. Will calls this a "fanaticism of sympathy." He thinks one should enjoy life whenever one can, and by this enjoyment one contributes happiness to the world. He also suggests that Dorothea is seeking martyrdom or self-punishment. Dorothea feels Will misunderstands, and argues that she is just idealistic and emotional. Will, who becomes very emotional, exclaims that Dorothea gives the impression of never having had any childhood and of suffering a great deal. He warns her that now she is going to Lowick to suffocate morally and aesthetically in the stifling, oppressive atmosphere of Casaubon's prison. Dorothea, in determined tone, asserts, "Lowick is my chosen home."

Comment

Ladislaw is unable to appreciate the idealism of Dorothea. Recall how Eliot stresses the obstacles which the realities of life place before idealists.

Dorothea, remembering what Will had said the other day about Casaubon's neglect of German scholarship, questions him as to the possibility of her husband's chances of succeeding without German information. Will answers slightingly. "How can you bear to speak so lightly?" Dorothea angrily asks. She also is beginning to understand the hopelessness of her husband's project, yet she defends him on the theory that "to fail grandly" is better than never to have made an attempt. Will, now concurring with this view, reveals his plan to forsake Casaubon's generosity by returning to England to become independent. He believes that Dorothea does not really love Casaubon, but her pride and stubbornness motivate her to serve him. He is ready to leave, apologizing to her for hurting her (by suggesting ideas for Casaubon's failure), but she expresses a fondness for him and wishes him success in his new venture. He offers his help to her if she ever needs it.

Later, Dorothea tells Casaubon of Will's new determination but he is interested only listlessly. At his request, Dorothea will not mention Will's name again. It is interesting to note that Casaubon uses terms of endearment only when his manner is "the coldest."

Comment

Dorothea is unwilling to betray her loyalty to Casaubon in the face of his probable failure as a scholar. Will Ladislaw's decision to return to England is not unmixed with an egotistical evaluation of his own abilities, not unlike the foolish pride which has blinded Casaubon to the truth about his scholarly failures.

MIDDLEMARCH

TEXTUAL ANALYSIS

BOOK THREE: WAITING FOR DEATH; CHAPTERS 23 - 33

CHAPTER TWENTY-THREE

Fred Vincy is in trouble. He is in debt to Mr. Bambridge, a horse dealer who had lent him one hundred sixty pounds, which he has squandered. Bambridge required security, so Fred had obtained a note with Caleb Garth's signature. As we know, Fred had felt sure of receiving a present from his uncle; he had also put faith in his ability to sell a horse for profit; if all failed, he had hoped to solicit money from his father. The Vincys all lived prodigally, but the thought of his mother's sorrow and his father's disagreeableness discouraged Fred's inclination to borrow there. To whom does one usually turn when in debt? Why, to a poor friend who is most likely to extend himself at a great risk. As Eliot states, "One must be poor to know the luxury of giving." So Fred turned to Caleb, who had a high opinion of Fred and was sure Fred would turn out well. The Vincys are socially prominent, so they feel "superior" to the Garths. There is a slight family connection between the families through

Featherstone's two marriages (the first to Mr. Garth's sister, and the second to Mrs. Vincy's sister). Mr. Garth had a business failure, but has managed through hard work to pay his debts and redeem himself well. According to Middlemarch society, however, he was of the "lower" class, regardless of his spotless character. The children of the two families have always enjoyed a close relationship and Fred holds Mr. Garth in high opinion. He wishes to repay the note as quickly as possible to keep Mr. Garth's respect for him. Mr. Garth is absorbed in work on Sir James Chettam's farm buildings, and has neglected to tell his wife of the signature on the note.

Fred, moreover, has failed his exams and his father is livid with rage over debts he has incurred at school. Mr. Vincy, knowing Fred to be Featherstone's favorite heir, however, curbs his disfavor. Fred is aware of his father's thinking. The time for the payment of the debt is near, and Fred is still short of the sum. Of the hundred pounds he has received from his uncle, he deposits eighty with his mother and loses the other twenty at billiards. He next devises the plan of setting out to the horse fair with experienced horsemen (Horrock the veterinarian and Bambridge), to obtain their advice indirectly. He withdraws the eighty pounds from his mother's safekeeping, then buys a horse, Diamond, from a farmer for thirty pounds and his horse as a swap. He mistakenly believes that it is a good buy. He intends to sell it at a profit to Lord Medlicote, who is in the market for a horse. Fred is on his way home with high hopes of reducing his debt to almost nothing.

Comment

The scene between Fred Vincy, Bambridge, and the others at the Houndsley horse fair shows Eliot's great skill in capturing with realistic details the affairs of rural English life in the nineteenth century.

CHAPTER TWENTY-FOUR

Diamond, while in his stall, displays a violent nature; after almost killing the groom, he proceeds to lame himself by catching his leg in a rope. Now Fred has but fifty pounds and with the note due in five days, little prospect of increasing his capital. Normally, Fred would have procrastinated in hope of Providence's providing a way out, but his love for Mary and respect for Caleb urge him to face up to the situation. Nevertheless, Fred is despondent, thinking of the interviews ahead. Mr. Garth is not in his office, so Fred proceeds to the Garth home. The family is a happy one and Fred is quite at home there. There are four boys and two girls, including Mary. It is a simple home, with nothing rich except love and hospitality. Mrs. Garth is a sensible, patient, good-natured woman who accepts what is unalterable and understands, loves, and helps Caleb. She is fond of Fred in a motherly way, and often excuses his follies. She is busily teaching grammar and baking when Fred arrives. Mrs. Garth has saved ninety-two pounds for her son Alfred's education. When Fred hears this news, he is ashamed. Mr. Garth arrives; Fred tells him of the situation-much to the surprise of Mrs. Garth, who had been uninformed. With the Christmas holidays approaching, Mr. Garth is worried about his financial situation, but Mrs. Garth offers her ninety-two pounds and pledges money of Mary's for the rest. She realizes that Caleb is crushed and gently reprimands him; first, for not telling her about the note and, second, for being so charitable as to perform work often for nothing. However, with Mrs. Garth's ninety-two pounds and Mary's money they will meet the note.

Caleb had been fascinated by the land at an early age; apprenticed to a surveyor, he came to know more of management, building, and mining than most professionals. He considers it to be highly dignified work and he is most happy and at peace doing it; however he cannot manage his own money, with the result that he runs his family into constant financial difficulty.

Comment

George Eliot's father was an estate manager, whose duties were like those of Caleb Garth. Witness the sympathetic treatment of Caleb's inability to manage his money, and the emphasis that the Garth family places on love and respect in preference to mere affluence.

CHAPTER TWENTY-FIVE

Fred wants to visit Mary before Caleb arrives to tell her that she will have to give him the part of her savings pledged by her mother. She is at Stone Court. Fred is remorseful, "I am a good-for-nothing blackguard scoundrel." Mary begins to cry when he tells her about the debt. He asks Mary to ask his uncle for a loan to send her brother Alfred to school, but Mary refuses flatly: the Garths do not beg. Fred pleads that he is merely unfortunate like other men often are, and uses Mr. Garth's bankruptcy as an example. Mary is incensed; she replies that her father lost his money by thinking of work to be done for others, not following his own idle pleasure. When Fred asks forgiveness, Mary candidly asks him if he thinks forgiveness will restore the lost money. Fred promises to reform and to become anything she wants him to be, if she will say she loves him. Mary becomes somewhat more tender with him, but not to the point of complete forgiveness.

After Fred leaves, Caleb arrives and informs Mary of the debt. She offers him twenty-four pounds although he needs only eighteen; he proceeds to warn Mary of Fred's well-intentioned but useless ways. Young people often get married with illusions and soon enough find that it is much harder than they imagined, explains Garth. Mary reassures him that she "will never engage herself to one who has no independence and who goes on loitering away his time on the chance that others will provide for him."

CHAPTER TWENTY-SIX

On his way home, Fred becomes ill. His mother calls for Dr. Wrench (a small;, neat, bilious man, with a well-dressed wig), who tells him he has a "slight derangement." He distributes the usual ineffective drugs, and when Fred attempts to carry on his usual routine after a few days, he becomes worse. Dr. Wrench cannot be found. Rosamond sees Dr. Lydgate passing by, and implores her mother to call him. Lydgate tells them that Fred has typhoid fever in its early stages and puts him on complete bedrest. Mrs. Vincy is distraught, but vents her displeasure about Dr. Wrench's neglect. She wants Lydgate to continue attending Fred. Her husband is also angry with Wrench, yet is more annoyed at the "inconvenience" caused by Fred's fever. Lydgate is now the family doctor for the Vincy family. Dr. Wrench does not take his dismissal from the case kindly; he is inclined to place the blame upon Lydgate for the whole situation, since he is a younger man with less experience.

CHAPTER TWENTY-SEVEN

Fred is delirious and Mrs. Vincy pleads with Lydgate to "save him." Rosamond cooperates with the doctor to calm her mother. When Fred's crisis passes, Lydgate finds himself thinking more of Rosamond. According to her "theory" of love-that close proximity breeds love-this opportunity for prolonged contact should prove fruitful. After the quarantine is lifted, Lydgate decides that a little harmless flirtation with Rosamond will enliven their relationship. To Rosamond, however, flirtation is a sign of love. She feels he is far superior to her other admirers: he wears the right clothes, is knowledgeable on various subjects, and has the proper manners and accent of a university man. She sees only the facade of the man, and Lydgate sees only her beauty, cleverness, and amiability.

Lydgate, however, has made enemies in Middlemarch, although it has been unintentional on his part. One in particular is Mr. Ned Plymdale, who is seeking Rosamond's affection but has been rebuffed. He becomes jealous of the time Rosamond spends with Lydgate; Rosamond thinks that she and Lydgate are practically "engaged." That evening Lydgate still seems to be more interested in his study of primitive tissue; he also senses an imminent feud with the other medical men, especially when Bulstrode's plans for managing the new hospital are announced.

CHAPTER TWENTY-EIGHT

Reverend and Mrs. Casaubon return home to Lowick Manor in the middle of January. It now seems to Dorothea that the house is smaller and more confining. The furniture seems to have shrunk; the books in the bookcase appear artificial.

Comment

Eliot uses images in the room's physical setting to evoke a mood. Dorothea's gloomy response to her home suggests that her hopes for success and happiness in her marriage have also shrunk.

Only Dorothea and the house's fire are aglow with life. She is anxious for her wifely duties to begin, so she may share her husband's destiny. She asks, "What shall I do?" "Whatever you please, my dear," answers Casaubon.

Dorothea is becoming a moral prisoner, as Will Ladislaw had prophesied. She is disenchanted; her religious fervor is a "solitary cry in the night." Casaubon, who is not feeling well, retires to the library. Mr. Brooke and Celia unexpectedly visit the Casaubons. Mr. Brooke does not see the disillusionment in Dorothea and mentions to her that her husband appears pale, a fact which she has failed to notice. Dorothea sees that her sister is blushing, and Celia finally reveals that she and Sir James Chettham are to be married. Dorothea is pleased; she tells Celia that she believes Sir James to be a "good, honorable man."

CHAPTER TWENTY-NINE

The chapter begins with an analysis of Casaubon's thoughts concerning his marriage. With all his frigidity of manner and speech, and lack of joy in most things not concerning his study, he still has an "intense consciousness" and is "spiritually a-hungered like the rest of us." His criteria for judging a woman's suitability for marriage were age (the younger the better), submissiveness, a social rank equal to his, moral principles, virtue, and understanding. Aware of his age and afraid he would miss the advantages of being married, he began to seek a wife. In Dorothea he had seen the perfect choice, viewing her also as a good potential secretary, although never considering her rights to happiness in marriage. He was doubtful of the power of his mind, but knew Dorothea believed he was capable of great work and was flattered. Scrupulous, and not blessed with a strong body, Casaubon is a sensitive man but too languid to feel or express enthusiasm about anything. Afraid to show his feelings to Dorothea, he now holds great misgivings about his own power as a scholar. He cannot experience any of the joys of life, since his chief concern is the preservation of his reputation for scholarship.

While Dorothea and Casaubon are at work in the library, he pauses to offer her a two-page letter from Will Ladislaw, remarking that he hopes that she does not ask Will to visit them, because he has no leisure "to waste" on Will. Dorothea is shocked and angry that he prejudges her and underestimates her concern for his privacy. Leaving Will's letter unread, she retires; a short time later he hears the slam of a book on the floor of the library. Casaubon has suffered a heart attack! Celia and Sir James arrive to visit the Casaubons. They send for Dr. Lydgate, who arrives promptly to attend to the stricken man.

CHAPTER THIRTY

Casaubon begins to recover after a few days. Dr. Lydgate advises moderation and variety of relaxation. He has planned to speak to Dorothea about her husband's condition; he is motivated by psychological as well as medical reasons. Dorothea beseeches him to tell her the truth about Casaubon. He advises that her he could live for fifteen years or that he could die suddenly. Casaubon is not to be informed of these possibilities because of the anxiety it might cause him. He tells her that above all else he must avoid consternation. Dorothea feels guilty about the letters from Will and her behavior in the library prior to her husband's attack.

She later reads Will's letters. He tells of his appreciation for the help given him by Casaubon; he is anxious to do well on his own in order to show that Casaubon's good faith was not in vain. He announces his arrival in England and his intention to visit them in order to deliver the picture of Casaubon (called "The Dispute), painted by Adolph Naumann. The other letter continues their discussion on art begun in Rome. Dorothea, afraid that this visit will cause excessive anxiety for her husband, asks her uncle to write to Will requesting him to postpone a visit to Lowick because of her husband's illness. As Mr. Brooke is writing the letter, he decides to invite Will to Tipton Grange. He has purchased the *Middlemarch Pioneer*, a newspaper he intends to use to further his political ambitions, and since Celia is leaving to marry, a young man with Will's potential will be pleasant to have working for him. Mr. Brooke, however, neglects to reveal this invitation to Dorothea.

CHAPTER THIRTY-ONE

Rosamond Vincy is elated when she thinks that Lydgate has now attended to two of the finest families of Middlemarch: Sir James Chettam's and Casaubon's. She feels it must be dreadful for Dorothea to have to live with a sick or dying man. Lydgate's frequent visits to Rosamond have given Middlemarch society something about to gossip, and Mrs. Bulstrode, who was never really satisfied with her sister's marriage, is now determined to see Rosamond's future husband become socially prominent. We find her frequenting the house of Mrs. Plymdale for the purpose of arranging a match with Ned Plymdale and her niece. Mrs. Plymdale believes that there is "something" between Rosamond and Dr. Lydgate. Mrs. Bulstrode is shocked to hear of their rumored engagement. She goes to visit her niece.

Mrs. Bulstrode confronts Rosamond with the rumor but Rosamond denies it, saying she cares little about social gossip. Her aunt reminds her that she is now twenty-two and will receive no fortune from her father. She attempts to discourage Rosamond's interest in Lydgate, giving the following reasons: he is poor; his profession is not well thought of in Middlemarch; and he has no real principles. Rosamond displays a calm but determined will to do what she has resolved. Mrs. Bulstrode warns Rosamond about the possible loss of the high style of living she is accustomed to and offers Ned Plymdale, a man, she suggests, who will be able to offer her everything she needs for marriage. Rosamond refuses him and affects a "tortured heroine" reaction.

Mrs. Bulstrode considers it is her duty to arrange a meeting with Lydgate to ask him about his intentions. She then tells him that he should not take up so much of Rosamond's time unless he intends to marry her. When Mr. Farebrother makes a remark about the romantic notions of the girls of Middlemarch concerning Lydgate, the doctor decides to visit the Vincy household only when necessary. Rosamond is very unhappy when she misses him for two days. She begins to feel the pangs of unrequited love, but she is not disposed to any desperate act. She does not know Lydgate's reasons for neglecting her and is, therefore, very cold to him when he makes a visit. She involuntarily begins to cry; Lydgate suddenly thinks that he does love her and wishes to marry her. They seek out Mr. Vincy, who gives his consent at once.

Comment

This last scene is conveyed by description and narrative comment. It achieves its effect by the way emotions are expressed chiefly by physical postures and gestures; only one line of dialogue is used. Lydgate asks Rosamond, "What is the matter? You are distressed. Tell me-pray." Her unusual naturalness has captured Lydgate; he becomes trapped into marriage and so ruins both their live. Only here and one other time, later in the novel, does Rosamond stop living in her fantasy world sufficiently to transcend her egoism. Ironically, as we shall see, the second time she saves Dorothea and Ladislaw. But it is not love which binds Lydgate to Rosamond; it is affection, tenderness, and his consciousness of having hurt her.

As Lydgate begins, so must he go on; he will be disillusioned; the beginning foreshadows the end. Unlike Casaubon, whose emotions are buried in a sealed tomb, we see that Lydgate's are in a sepulchre; it is not sealed; his are released at the slightest concussion.

An appropriate image used repeatedly by Eliot in this chapter is the "chain"-a symbol of entanglement, bonds, and fetters.

CHAPTER THIRTY-TWO

All of Peter Featherstone's greedy relatives become interested in his will when they realize that he is close to death. His brother Solomon and sister Jane are wealthy themselves, yet they are confident Peter will not overlook them; they think it natural that he should keep away his less-favored brother Jonah and sister Martha. The clan flocks to his house but Peter does not wish to see any of them. Mrs. Vincy is helping to advise the servants on how to handle the influx of relatives. Brother Jonah perches in the kitchen prepared to await his brother's death. (Notice the vulture image.) He watches Mary Garth with beady, suspicious eyes. She is much annoyed, and tells Fred of the spectacle; he howls with laughter, but attempts to relieve her distress through a verbal attack on the relatives. Brother Solomon and sister Jane Waule are there every day for hours. Dressed in black, they ignore Peter's orders and present themselves at the door, although he is enraged. They are very upset to see Mrs. Vincy and Fred, for fear that these two may have encouraged their brother to change his will in their favor. Featherstone's cousin Borthrop Trumbull (who is also his business advisor) takes a fancy Mary Garth, expecting that Peter will find it in his heart to be kind to her in his will. Solomon declares he does not care to whom Peter leaves his money as long as they deserve it. (This comment is directed at Mary.) Trumbull is suspected of knowing the contents of the will; Jane and Solomon attempt to learn its contents from him. He tells them nothing (he really does not know the contents) and enjoys watching their reaction. He tells Solomon that Mary is a sensible girl and "minds" what she is doing. Solomon retorts that one can wager Peter "has left that girl a lumping sum."

CHAPTER THIRTY-THREE

That night, after midnight, while Mary is sitting up with Featherstone, she thinks of how ridiculous his relatives are in pretending to be interested in his welfare. Mary has particular disdain for Mrs. Vincy's attitude about Fred, and she wonders how Fred will react if he is excluded from Peter's will, which she suspects is going to happen. At three o'clock, Featherstone calls her to his side and asks her how many relatives are in the house. He then tells her that they are all fools. He asserts that he knows what their motives are. He reveals that he has had two wills drawn up, and now wishes to burn one of them. Mary does not wish to be open to suspicion by helping him to do such an act, so he demands that she call Fred Vincy. Mary does not want to have Fred implicated, so she agrees to burn one of the wills, only if he will call Jonah and the others. He refuses; Mary then urges him to call a lawyer. Peter orders her to open a chest, and to remove the money in it. It is hers if she will oblige him; he avows that no one knows it is there. Mary refuses again. In anger Peter throws a stick at her, but it falls to the floor. Since dawn is rapidly approaching, Mary puts more wood on the fading fire. But before morning arrives, Peter Featherstone is dead.

MIDDLEMARCH

TEXTUAL ANALYSIS

BOOK FOUR: THREE LOVE PROBLEMS; CHAPTERS 34 - 42

CHAPTER THIRTY-FOUR

Peter Featherstone is buried on a cloudy and chilly morning in May. Word has spread that it is to be a "big burying"; old Featherstone had left directions to make sure he had a funeral "beyond his betters." He had loved to spend money on his peculiar tastes, but best of all he had loved to make people feel uncomfortable through the power of his money. He had arranged the funeral with imagination and certainly enjoyed the anticipation, foregoing, of course, the proceedings. The three mourning coaches are met by the clergyman, Mr. Cadwallader. Fred chose him instead of Casaubon, who was of his own parish, because Fred did not want to suffer through his sermon, Mrs. Cadwallader watches (with Celia and Sir James) from an upper window in their house at Lowick. Celia remarks that she can endure no more, but observes that Dorothea enjoys it because she likes melancholy things. Mr. Brooke arrives and comments that Casaubon has returned and is in the library studying.

Discussing the various people attending the funeral, they notice a man with whom they are not familiar. All are struck by his odd appearance: "... bulging eyes, a sort of frog-face...." Celia chides Dorothea about not telling her that Ladislaw had arrived. Mr. Brooke intervenes, explaining that Will is staying with him at the Grange, and that they have the picture of Casaubon painted in Rome by Adolf Naumann. Upon hearing the news, Casaubon remembers that he had not seen Will's letter when he became ill; he now concludes that Dorothea had asked her uncle to invite him to visit. When Dorothea realizes what her husband thinks has happened, she is disturbed but careful not to make a scene. In the meantime, Mr. Brooke has gone to meet Ladislaw.

CHAPTER THIRTY-FIVE

George Eliot compares the relatives at the reading of Peter Featherstone's will to the animals which gathered on Noah's Ark to "feed on the same store of fodder." The Featherstone blood has allied itself against the Vincys and Mary Garth. What disturbs them most of all is the strange-looking man seen at the funeral. Some have seen him before at Featherstone's but paid little attention to his presence. Now, in their greedy anxiety, they are even more concerned with the identity of the "frog-faced" man. Mr. Standish, the lawyer, expects to read the last of three wills he had drawn up for Mr. Featherstone. He is surprised to find only two wills. The first (and ineffectual) will, dated August 9, 1825, bequeathed ten thousand pounds to Fred Vincy; the land properties were to be given to Joshua Rigg, the frog-faced man. He was to be the sole executor and was to take the name Featherstone. The greedy relatives were to receive small sums.

But there is a second (and valid) will dated March 1, 1826, and a codicil (additional) to this will.

This will was the one the dying Featherstone wanted Mary Garth to burn. Mr. Standish is told to read the second will. It revokes the bequests to all but Rigg, who is to receive "all the land lying in Lowick parish, with all the stock and household furniture." The remainder is to be used for the construction of Featherstone's Alms-Houses for old men.

Comment

Disappointed and indignant, all of Featherstone's relatives now reveal their true dislike for him. Fred feels ill from the reading of the will, for Featherstone's second will was probably written to punish Fred for borrowing money.

Mary tells Fred he is better off without the money. Fred childishly fears he cannot repay the money which Caleb and Mary used to pay his note; now he must go into the ministry. Mary will have to seek another job to support herself.

Comment

Another stranger, Joshua Rigg, has come to Middlemarch; although he is a "visible thorn," no one yet knows what his plans are.

CHAPTER THIRTY-SIX

Mr. Vincy's outlook changes now that Fred has been left nothing; he warns Fred that he had better pass his examinations. Fred who only twenty-four hours ago had expectations of paying his debts and becoming a gentleman of leisure, is crushed completely. He was sure Mary would have married him once he inherited the money.

Mr. Vincy refuses to give his consent for Rosamond to marry Lydgate, because he "hasn't a farthing." Mrs. Vincy is distressed because Rosamond has already begun preparations for the wedding; moreover, Mr. Bulstrode favors the match. Rosamond dismisses discussion of financial matters, particularly any mention of a dowry to Lydgate, yet she makes lavish preparations for their home. Mr. Vincy does not discuss matters with Lydgate, preferring to play the gratuitous host, whom no one criticizes. Lydgate continues to spend most of his evenings at their home. He and Rosamond continue to spin their "gossamer web." She finally reveals her father's objections to the marriage. Lydgate tells her that if she is unhappy at home they should hasten their marriage. They agree on a date six weeks hence and begin to make plans for their home and for the wedding journey. Mr. Vincy makes certain that Lydgate has insured his life. Rosamond wrangles a promise from Lydgate that he will bring her to Quallingham, the home of his titled uncle Godwin, for a visit. She also hopes that he will find employment elsewhere than in Middlemarch.

CHAPTER THIRTY-SEVEN

Comment

In the beginning of this chapter, George Eliot discusses the political situation of the era. George IV is dead. The cry for reform is upon the land-Tory leaders themselves are in favor of liberal measures, such as the Catholic Emancipation Act and the Reform Bill. Such Tory stalwarts as the Duke of Wellington and Lord Grey are enthusiastically pushing for reform; only the House of Lords threatens to block these measures. At this point Lord Grey persuades King William IV (1830-1837), to threaten the creation by royal prerogative of enough new Whig peers to put the Reform Bill through the House of Lords. It is finally passed on June 4, 1832.

Will is anxious to work on the Middlemarch newspaper; he goes to see Dorethea not only to ask advice, but to visit her as well. Casaubon has gone to see the archdeacon; Dorothea is alone. Will tells her of the offer and she later tells her husband of Will's visit. He shows much displeasure. Later that evening, he writes a letter to Will expressing his objections to Will's taking a job with Mr. Brooke.

Because Dorothea spends so much time alone, she has the opportunity to think of the family's poor treatment of Will's grandmother. She was cut off from the family inheritance and from family protection because her family did not approve of the man she married. Dorothea thinks this situation should be righted, and she mentions it to her husband, suggesting that he make provision in his will to give his cousin Will half of his estate. Casaubon becomes enraged; he forbids Dorothea to mention the matter again.

The following day, Casaubon receives a reply from Will; it tells him that he intends to take the job with Mr. Brooke, regardless of the objections of his benefactor. Casaubon is filled with disgust and suspicion, but can turn to no one for advice because he is distrustful of everyone's feelings toward him. He remains silent.

CHAPTER THIRTY-EIGHT

Sir James Chettam is dissatisfied with Mr. Brooke's interest in politics. He goes to visit the Cadwalladers because discussion of this upsets Celia. They believe Mr. Brooke's campaign will result in failure. Rumors are that Ladislaw is "a quill-driving alien, a foreign emissary, and what not." In discussing the good and bad points of Mr. Brooke's decision, Mr. Cadwallader thinks that a loss may make him more conscious of the management of his estate. Sir James reflects that the management of his estate would improve only if he were to rehire Caleb Garth, whom he had fired twelve years earlier.

Mr. Brooke enters, and the group discusses with him the highly critical article written about him in the town's rival newspaper The Trumpet. The article suggests that "a certain landlord" (Brooke) advocates reform methods for other farms, but does little regarding his own, farm except to collect the rents. Brooke believes that the people of Middlemarch are backward and need to be educated. They all agree that if a man decides to enter public life, he must be willing to accept the attendant consequences, which often take the form of ridicule and involve expense.

Comment

Mr. Brooke, like Dorothea and Dr. Lydgate, will discover that one's ideas and ambitions, however worthy in themselves, are always subject to the harsh realities of everyday existence.

CHAPTER THIRTY-NINE

Sir James thinks Dorothea could dissuade her uncle from entering politics and instead concentrate on making reforms in the management of his estate. He arranges for her to meet Brooke at the Grange. Mr. Brooke tells her that he hopes she is not getting too "learned" for a woman. Dorothea "pours forth" her emotions, telling him of how he might make vast improvements in his estate. He is stunned to realize how much help she could be, but decides to ignore her advice.

Will Ladislaw takes this opportunity to tell Dorothea of his correspondence with Reverend Casaubon, who forbade him to visit his home again. Dorothea feels wretched; she thinks her husband is completely wrong.

After his visit with Dorothea, Mr. Brooke finds it necessary to make an infrequent visit to one of his tenants, a man named Dagley. The man speaks loudly and disrespectfully to Mr. Brooke, who is astonished to find that he is not as popular a landlord as he had believed.

Comment

The tenant Dagley has a dog who is as disagreeable as his master. Eliot uses both to symbolize the bitter anger of English farmers caused by the agricultural depression and the resulting penury of the farms.

CHAPTER FORTY

This chapter returns us to Caleb Garth and his family. Mary Garth must look for a new position after the death of Peter Featherstone. She has decided to go to York to teach, although she is not fond of schoolrooms. While they are eating breakfast, Caleb opens a letter he has received from Sir James, requesting that he manage Brooke's estates. It will be a position with more than adequate pay; Mary will not have to leave. His wife considers the offer a blessing.

The vicar of St. Botolph's, Mr. Farebrother, pays a visit to the family that evening. He wishes to see not only Caleb and his wife, but Mary also. He tells them that he has come as an envoy of Fred Vincy, who has been out of town at school for many months. The vicar remarks that Fred is trying again for his degree, although he does not wish to enter the ministry. The couple agrees that he should not enter the church.

CHAPTER FORTY-ONE

The transactions between Mr. Bulstrode and Mr. Joshua Rigg Featherstone for the sale of certain property at Stone Court begin. (Notice the name added to "Rigg," a condition required in Peter Featherstone's will.) Joshua is, as always, "sleek, neat, and cool as the frog he resembled." He had been brought up in a seaport town and had been educated in small commercial houses at the seaport. He has little respect for the rural Featherstones.

We are introduced to a new character, John Raffles, Joshua's stepfather. He is nearly sixty, stout of figure, and swaggering of air; his hair is thick, curly, and graying. The avaricious Raffles is interested in his stepson's wealth, but Joshua remembers Raffle's cruel treatment and neglect of him as a child. He therefore refuses to do more than provide a small weekly dole to Raffles' wife as long as Raffles is alive. He fears that Raffles will seize any large sum he might give her. Instead of showing defeat, Raffles good-naturedly asks for a drink and his carfare to return. He then observes, "There's nothing I like better than plaguing you."

Raffles puts his brandy flask in his pocket. He picks up a piece of paper which has fallen to the ground and shoves it under the flask (which fits loosely in his pocket), in order to hold it firm.

> Comment

Unknown to Raffles, the piece of paper he has picked up to use to steady his brandy flask is a letter from Mr. Bulstrode. This letter contains significant information about Bulstrode's past; as we shall see, Raffles will want money to remain silent about the information contained in this letter.

CHAPTER FORTY-TWO

Dr. Lydgate, upon returning from his honeymoon, is requested to schedule his visits so as to include Reverend Casaubon. The Reverend, instead of assembling his notes and writing the "Key to All Mythologies," has something else on his mind which makes him inquisitive about his real state of health. Will Ladislaw haunts him; Dorothea seems to "judge" him. Although she is a model wife, Casaubon is suspicious of her ardent nature; when she is silent he mistakes it for a suppressed rebellion. Hadn't she asked her uncle to invite Will? Hadn't she requested that he should give Ladislaw half of his estate?

Casaubon requests Dr. Lydgate to reveal to him the whole truth about his illness. He wants to know its nature and his chances for the future. Finally, Lydgate admits that death can be sudden in illnesses such as his. After the doctor's departure, Casaubon rebuffs Dorothea. He secretly envisions her marrying Will after his death. He becomes reconciled with her, however, after spending time alone in the library. He treats her kindly and says, "Come my dear, come. You are young and need not extend your life by watching."

Comment

This utterance is the closest to real feeling that Casaubon will ever make to Dorothea.

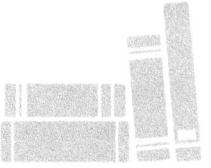

MIDDLEMARCH

TEXTUAL ANALYSIS

BOOK FIVE: THE DEAD HAND; CHAPTERS 43 - 53

CHAPTER FORTY-THREE

Dorothea is anxious to learn everything about her husband's illness and the concern it is causing him, lest she offend him unknowingly. She visits Dr. Lydgate but he is not at home. Rosamond in there, for Dorothea hears her playing music; a man's voice can also be heard. When they meet, both women are anxious to appraise one another. As they are talking, much to the delightful surprise of Dorothea, Will Ladislaw steps forth and offers to fetch Dr. Lydgate, who is busy at the new hospital. Realizing how displeased Casaubon would be with this scene, Dorothea declines Will's offer and decides to seek the doctor herself. She reflects on the preceding events, thinking it improper that Will should remain with Rosamond in her husband's absence. She begins to sob: her image of Will is slightly spoiled. He, also, is humiliated because he senses that Dorothea does not approve of his presence with Rosamond.

Will tells Rosamond how he worships Dorothea and thinks of her as a "perfect woman." Later, Rosamond tells her husband about Dorothea's visit and Will's remarks to her about Dorothea. Lydgate remarks that Ladislaw is a "poor devil" for adoring Dorothea.

Comment

With his comment about Ladislaw, Lydgate reveals his own weakness in marriage. He lacks the strength needed to speak out against his wife's expenditures, although he realizes that he cannot now devote his full energies to his work.

CHAPTER FORTY-FOUR

Dorothea visits Dr. Lydgate at the New Hospital and learns that there is no change in her husband's condition. The doctor takes this opportunity to question Dorothea about her awareness of the hospital's needs. She is very interested because, for the first time since her marriage, she sees an opportunity to be "useful." Dr. Lydgate explains that through Mr. Bulstrode's efforts and money, projects are making great strides, but some of the medical men and a few others are causing a disturbance. Lydgate feels their opposition is due partly to their dislike of Bulstrode and partly to their jealousy.

Comment

The immediate motive for the opposition is that Bulstrode has placed the medical directorship in Lydgate's hands.

Dr. Lydgate explains that regardless of opposition and personal inconvenience, he will continue fighting for the benefit of science and the medical profession. Bulstrode can be of great help to Lydgate's projects, and so he sees no harm in cooperating with Bulstrode to achieve these ends. Dorothea is grateful to Dr. Lydgate for his information and praises him for his high ideals. She wishes she could "awake every morning" with the satisfying knowledge of her value and service to the world. Later, she asks her husband if she may donate two hundred pounds a year to the New Hospital. Casaubon agrees. Without questioning her about her interview with Lydgate, he remains distrustful of her affections.

CHAPTER FORTY-FIVE

Comment

The bulk of this chapter shows us (as the reactions of people to Dr. Lydgate are reported), a cross-section of nineteenth-century English characters, particularly those in the medical profession.

Lydgate and Bulstrode view the opposition to the New Hospital in different lights. Lydgate considers it a mixture of jealousy and prejudice; Bulstrode sees it as a personal vendetta prompted by the distrust of the people and their hatred of his ministerial views and affiliation. Most of the gossip is repetitious but it is heard from all social levels: from the conservative Dr. Minchen to the superstitious Mrs. Dollop, the landlady of the Tankard in Slaughter Land. (The latter is convinced that Dr. Lydgate wishes to kill patients for purposes of experimentation and research!) But Lydgate quickly develops lines of friendship and loyalty to overcome the early distrust and opposition.

Comment

Dr. Lydgate has incurred the dislike of several Middlemarch doctors because:

1. He sees little value in the dispensing of various medicines. His patients therefore correctly assume that they have long been paying money for worthless drugs.

2. He has effected certain cures which Middlemarchers consider miraculous; such cures reflect unfavorably on other doctors who earlier misdiagnosed the illnesses.

Bulstrode is anxious to solicit as much money as possible for maintaining the hospital, because he has designs on land tracts, and realizes that substantial capital will be needed to purchase them. His plan for management of the hospital is:

1. The hospital is to be reserved for fevers of all kinds.

2. Lydgate is to be chief medical superintendent.

3. Lydgate is to hold the power of ultimate decision, which is to be irrevocable.

4. General management is to be in the hands of five directors associated with Bulstrode.

5. Members are to be replaced by the board itself.

6. Votes are to be allotted in proportion to the amount of contributions given.

All the medical men refuse to visit the new hospital, but Lydgate plans to bring in new doctors; Bulstrode backs his plan to organize a board of members who are in sympathy with them and who will go along with their demands. In a conversation with Reverend Farebrother, Lydgate is warned that he should not become obligated to Bulstrode; he should disassociate himself as much as possible. Farebrother also cautions him not to go too deeply into debt.

CHAPTER FORTY-SIX

New political activity in *Middlemarch* is apparent with the increased interest in the Reform Bill then being debated in Parliament. Mr. Brooke hopes that the election of a new party will help his chances of winning a seat in Parliament. He and Will Ladislaw discuss what they believe are the most important aspects of reform; and Will becomes a noticeable figure in the town through his editorials and his speeches. No one in town knows that he is Casaubon's nephew. Lydgate disagrees with Will on Mr. Brooke's qualifications and on the Reform Bill. Many heated arguments ensue between Lydgate and Ladislaw. Rosamond and Lydgate are expecting a baby. Although he seems to have an avid interest in politics, Lydgate is actually more concerned with his own finances and his inability to pay a furniture bill. Wishing to save Rosamond from worry, however, he remains silent about his money problems.

CHAPTER FORTY-SEVEN

Ladislaw, sitting alone in his room, reflects about his life since he has returned to Middlemarch, for he is now unsure whether he has been wise in associating himself with Middlemarch, Mr. Brooke, and The Pioneer. Although he is devoted to Dorothea, he is somehow pleased that she is "unattainable." (He does not wish for Casaubon's death, as Casaubon suspects.) Ladislaw seems to enjoy the situation as it now is: he idealizes Dorothea but subconsciously is afraid that in reality she will disappoint his image should their relationship become any more personal.

The next morning Will decides to go to Lowick to church, just to see Dorothea. He knows he will be breaking Casaubon's commandment that he never visit again and seems to delight in the prospect of displeasing his uncle. At church, Will sees Dorothea, but he begins to feel uncomfortable when Casaubon enters, and soon: "utterly ridiculous, out of temper, and miserable." Dorothea appears as if she were repressing tears, probably from embarrassment. She and Casaubon leave the church without glancing back.

Comment

Eliot draws a sharp contrast in this chapter between the way one pictures an event in one's imagination and the disappointing way the event occurs in reality.

CHAPTER FORTY-EIGHT

Distressed over the disagreement between her husband and Will, Dorothea senses that Will's appearance at church has eliminated any hope for a reconciliation between them, which she has secretly hoped for. Although Casaubon has some difficulty breathing and is annoyed about the incident, he continues to work diligently on his notebooks. Dorothea, because she lacks the comfort and love of a genuine human relationship, longs for companionship. She had found it to some degree in Will Ladislaw, but now he is gone and she is left with Casaubon's indifference and his stale scholarship. Before they retire, Casaubon solicits Dorothea's help in the library. He awakes in the middle of the night, complaining of difficulty in lying down. Dorothea reads to him, and he tells her feverishly to "mark" this or that. He seems to cover his material quicker than usual. Before going to sleep he tries to elicit a promise from her to carry out his "wishes" in the event of his death. She does not give him an answer because she believes that he might expect her to read through the vast amount of notes he has been taking. She understands now that he has clung to her knowing that only through her can he ever hope to publish his work. Yet she would devote herself to him and his work if he lived for another fifteen years-so why shouldn't she now promise to serve him in that capacity after his death? Dorothea hesitates. Perhaps, she fears, he wants something more, since he will not tell her what his wish is.

The night passes. Dorothea finally relents to herself and promises to give her husband an answer. When she goes to tell him, she finds him sitting with his head resting on his arms on a stone table. She speaks to him. But Dorothea never gives her answer. Casaubon is dead.

CHAPTER FORTY-NINE

Mr. Brooke and Sir James Chettam discuss Casaubon's will in the library at Lowick Grange. In a codicil (addition) to the will, in a rage of jealousy, Casaubon had stated that Dorothea was to forfeit the money left do her in the will if she ever married Will Ladislaw. Both men are shocked by this revelation and decide to protect Dorothea by keeping the contents of the will from her and by "protecting" her from Ladislaw.

Comment

Mr. Brooke is responsible for the second suggestion because he cannot afford to lose Will now that he has proven himself an able assistant to him in his campaign for Parliament.

CHAPTER FIFTY

Dorothea is visiting her sister Celia and her new baby at Freshitt Hall. She is considering what action to take as the new owner of Lowick Manor, and tells her uncle that she wishes to return to the Manor to go through her husband's papers to discover what plans he may have made regarding the house. He urges her to wait, but she is impatient. Inadvertently, Celia tells her sister of the secret codicil. Dorothea is shocked, because she had never considered Will in the light that Casaubon had presented him, and now suddenly recognizes a strange longing towards Will. She returns to Lowick Manor to seek any personal message Casaubon may have left for her, but after a thorough search of his papers, she finds nothing.

Lydgate speaks to Dorothea of Mr. Farebrother as a possible candidate for the position vacated by her husband. (Lydgate wants to purge his conscience for the vote he had cast against Farebrother.) Dorothea questions his habit of gambling, but Lydgate thinks that Farebrother, given a little security, would give it up entirely. When Lydgate leaves, Dorothea abandons herself to thoughts of Will Ladislaw.

CHAPTER FIFTY-ONE

Parliament has been dissolved and election fever is high. Will has not seen Dorothea since the death of her husband. He has been working long hours at the newspaper for the forthcoming election. Mr. Brooke is running on the independent ticket and is jubilant; not even heavy expenses can daunt his enthusiasm. Ladislaw continues to pound the best arguments for Reform into the tangled mind of Mr. Brooke. Before the day of nomination, Brooke must explain his views to the electors. He is confident, for his reforms as a landlord have silenced the blasts of the Trumpet, and he hears himself cheered a little as he drives into town. He and his friends stop at the Green Dragon and Brooke, normally a nondrinker, has two glasses of sherry. He begins his speech well but the effect of the sherry causes him to muddle his train of thought. As he speaks, someone in the throng raises an effigy of his exact likeness. A parrotlike voice begins echoing his words and the crowd begins to laugh and to throw eggs. It is obvious that the candidacy of Brooke is an inglorious failure.

Comment

A political maneuver by Brooke's enemies combined with his own foolish drinking have brought about his defeat. Eliot suggests that the police may have been bribed to ignore the planned disruption of Brooke's speech. This chapter is valuable for its insights into provincial English politics.

Will is dejected and resolves to give up The Pioneer and Mr. Brooke. He plans to work earnestly at political writing and speaking, for which he has a talent. When he is established, he will come back to see Dorothea. She must not know his reason for not wishing to marry her now.

Mr. Brooke, in a roundabout manner, makes it evident that he, among others, wishes Will to "quit" The Pioneer and to leave Middlemarch. "I shall go of my own movement," thinks Will Ladislaw.

CHAPTER FIFTY-TWO

Dorothea asks Reverend Farebrother and his family to be the tenants at Lowick Manor. They are delighted. His sister suggests to the clergyman that now he is in a position to marry and Mary Garth would be a good choice. He advises her that a wife is not to be chosen "as poultry in a market." He does, however, promise them that he will forego his card playing.

A week later, Fred Vincy, who has received his degree from Omnibus College, comes to visit Farebrother. He tells him that he does not want to enter the church, but he does not know what else he might be able to do. He also confesses his love for Mary Garth to the vicar. He then asks him to speak to her for him! Although Farebrother is in love with Mary himself, he goes to her with Fred's request.

When he sees Mary, he praises Fred's sincerity and good nature; wisdom, he says, lies in these two qualities. He also tells her not to feel guilt for not burning Peter Featherstone's second will because, according to law, if the second were destroyed, the first would be of no consequence. He also tells Mary that Fred has received his degree and will comply with the wishes of his father, if she will forgive his previous actions and state her feelings about him. Unhesitatingly, Mary says she will not marry him if he becomes a clergyman, because she feels that Fred is totally unfitted for such a vocation; she has no respect for men who use the cloth to better their social position. She will marry Fred only when he proves himself to be a responsible person. Mary detects an emotional tremor in the vicar's voice, but dismisses a romantic thought as foolish folly. Farebrother leaves, reflecting that he has never performed a more difficult duty.

Comment

Eliot employs dramatic **irony** effectively in this chapter. The reader is aware that Farebrother is genuinely interested in marrying Mary Garth, yet he is placed in a position of speaking to her of another's love for her. Every word of Mary's about Fred has special meaning for Farebrother, which only he and the reader can perceive.

CHAPTER FIFTY-THREE

Joshua Rigg surprises everyone by selling Stone Court to Mr. Bulstrode, thereby giving him even greater power in Middlemarch. Joshua's real ambition is to become a moneychanger. Peter Featherstone's relatives are delighted to hear the news, because they consider the dead man's wishes as expressed in his will to have been ignored.

Bulstrode is discussing stable drainage with Caleb Garth when a man in black rides forward to join them. The stranger is John Raffles, an acquaintance whom Bulstrode has not seen for twenty-five year. Garth leaves Bulstrode suddenly turns pale, because he knows Raffles is familiar with events in his past life.

Comment

At this point, Eliot summarizes past incidents to show the significance Raffles' appearance has for Bulstrode. Years earlier, Bulstrode had married an elderly, wealthy widow, whose daughter, Sarah, had run away from home with her small baby. A search had been made for them and Raffles, discovering their whereabouts, had been paid by Bulstrode to remain silent. He sent Raffles to America and had inherited his wife's money when she died.

Bulstrode gives Raffles two hundred pounds "blackmail" hoping he will leave Middlemarch. Bulstrode's present wife and Middlemarch society know nothing of his earlier disreputable actions. Raffles remembers the name of Bulstrode's stepdaughter. It is "Ladislaw"; Will Ladislaw is her son! Bulstrode fears that he will see John Raffles again.

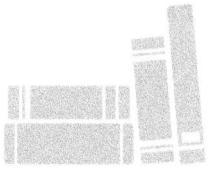

MIDDLEMARCH

TEXTUAL ANALYSIS

BOOK SIX: THE WIDOW AND THE WIFE; CHAPTERS 54 - 62

CHAPTER FIFTY-FOUR

After Dorothea has been at Freshitt for three months, she becomes increasingly restless; over the objections of Celia, Sir James, and Mrs. Cadwallader, she makes plans to return to Lowick. Upon her return, she realizes that her real reason for returning to Lowick Manor is to see Will Ladislaw.

One morning, Will makes a call on her. They both appear uncomfortable but determined in their conversation. He tells her that he has come to say goodbye because he is leaving to start a new life in London. She thinks that he must know of the codicil to the will, then tells him that she will never forget him. Before they are able to say anything else about their true feelings, Sir James enters. Will leaves immediately, after bidding Dorothea goodbye.

CHAPTER FIFTY-FIVE

Dorothea is unaware that she has experienced the emotion called love. She feels she will never see Ladislaw again, and makes some firm resolutions for the future.

Comment

Dorothea resolves that she will never remarry and will devote her time, money, and energy to the pursuit of happiness for others less fortunate than herself.

On a visit to Freshitt, Sir James, Celia, and Mrs. Cadwallader entreat Dorothea to remove her mourning cap. When she does, they exclaim about her beauty. Mrs. Cadwallader again approaches Dorothea on the subject of marriage and Dorothea reminds her that she is interested only in the idea of organizing a utopian society; she has consulted Mr. Garth about her plans. Sir James cannot think of Dorothea's remarrying either. He considers such an idea degrading and privately wishes her to choose solitude.

Comment

Dorothea is learning to substitute ideals for the love and happiness which a marriage to Will Ladislaw could have brought her.

CHAPTER FIFTY-SIX

Dorothea's interest in the building of cottages is renewed, especially because of her confidence in Caleb Garth and his approval of her ideas. She finds him to be the man best suited to manage her land at Lowick Manor.

Railroads are now being built through the smaller towns and villages. They are looked on up by many as being dangerous. The discussion of them is "as exciting a topic as the Reform Bill or the imminent horrors of cholera." One day, Peter Featherstone's brother, Solomon, is responsible for an uprising of tenant farmers against the railroad employees. Caleb Garth is having difficulty calming the angry farmers; just then, Fred Vincy offers to assist him. By coincidence, they both see in this effort a chance to improve their relationship; for Fred in particular, it is a way to prove himself to Mary.

Fred and Caleb, however, are the only members of both families pleased with Fred. Mrs. Garth fears that he may never become trustworthy. Mr. Vincy still thinks that Fred should enter the church.

CHAPTER FIFTY-SEVEN

That evening, Fred visits Lowick parsonage to call on Mrs. Garth. He assures her that he can be trusted to do a good job as Caleb's assistant. Even with Fred's reassurance, Mrs. Garth insists that Reverend Farebrother would be a better husband for Mary. Fred fails to realize that Mrs. Garth still looks unfavorably on him;

he hopes, after he proves himself, that he will finally win Mary. Mary has secretly decided to marry Fred and to refuse Reverend Farebrother, who has declared his own interest to her.

CHAPTER FIFTY-EIGHT

Captain Lydgate, a cousin of the doctor, pays a visit to the home of Lydgate and Rosamond. He persuades her, against her husband's wishes, to go horseback riding; as a result, her baby is born prematurely and dies.

Having incurred numerous bills until he owes a total debt of three hundred and eighty pounds, Lydgate begins to worry more about his financial situation. Rosamond finally realizes that they are under increasing strain but refuses to halt her prodigal spending. When she suggests that Lydgate ask her father for money, he becomes enraged, although he forgives her almost immediately. Lydgate looks sadly forward, "with dread to the inevitable future discussion about expenditures and the necessity for a complete change in their way of living."

CHAPTER FIFTY-NINE

Because gossip in a small town spreads rapidly, it is not long before Rosamond hears of the codicil to Casaubon's will forbidding any marriage between Dorothea and Will. Although warned by Lydgate not to mention it to Will, she reveals it to him. He had not known of it until this time. He calls it a "foul insult" both to Dorothea and himself; in anger, he tells Rosamond he will never marry Dorothea. Rosamond is concerned both with Will's anger toward her and with Lydgate's debts.

CHAPTER SIXTY

At the end of August, Mr. Bulstrode requests Will to judge the value of a painting he wishes to buy at an auction. Will agrees, using this request as an excuse for delaying his departure to London. During the bidding, a red faced man with whiskers steps in front of Will and asks if his mother's name was Sarah Dunkirk. The stranger, who is Mr. Raffles, appears to have accurate knowledge of Will's family, although Will has never seen him before. Raffles tells Will that he once knew his father and mother. He also reveals to Will that his mother ran away from home when she was a "young lass." Will stumbles away from Raffles in his confusion over the information he has been given about his mother. He is certain, however that there could be nothing dishonorable about her behavior.

Comment

A colorful picture of an English country auction is presented in this chapter. It is also a key **episode** in the plot, because of Will's conversation with Raffles.

CHAPTER SIXTY-ONE

Raffles comes to Mr. Bulstrode's house; when he finds that he is not at home, he leaves abruptly. Realizing that the revelation of his past life will make him the object of scorn in Middlemarch, Bulstrode feels powerless to help himself. In a flashback, he sees himself as a young banker's clerk. He had become close friends with Mr. Dunkirk, the richest man in the congregation of the church. Eventually he became a confidential accountant in

Mr. Dunkirk's pawnbroking business. He soon discovered that the business was receiving stolen goods, but he neither made an effort to leave, nor to do anything about it. He rationalized his part in the operation by saying that it was part of a divine plan. Years later, both Mr. Dunkirk and his only son died, leaving Mrs. Dunkirk alone, except for a daughter Sarah who ran away from home to go on the stage. Her decision was made when she realized the nature of her father's "business." Sarah had never been found. Bulstrode and the widow planned to marry but she refused until she had made a final search for her daughter. Sarah was found by Raffles, but the information was never revealed to Mrs. Dunkirk. The only persons who shared the secret were Bulstrode and Raffles, who was paid for keeping silent and remaining out of sight. Bulstrode married the widow Dunkirk, and subsequently became heir to all of her wealth when she died five years later.

Comment

Mrs. Dunkirk's lost daughter, Sarah, was the mother of Will Ladislaw. He, therefore, is the proper heir to the Dunkirk fortune.

Bulstrode goes to visit Will and reveals their connection. In order to prevent a scandal, he offers Will five hundred pounds a year and a share in his own estate after his death. Will speaks scornfully to Bulstrode. He tells him he wants no part of any money that was made dishonestly.

CHAPTER SIXTY-TWO

After leaving Bulstrode, Will plans to pay a final visit to Dorothea and then to leave Middlemarch. He writes a note to her, but she is not at home when it arrives. Sir James, because of his hatred for Will, has been spreading rumors of the friendship between Will and Rosamond Lydgate. Dorothea defends Will against the gossip but when she accidently meets him at Tipton Grange and discovers that he is leaving for good, she wonders if he fears possible involvement with Rosamond. Dorothea fails to realize that it is because of her alone that he has made his choice. Will's final words, however, reassure her that he loves her truly. He leaves Middlemarch the following evening.

MIDDLEMARCH

TEXTUAL ANALYSIS

BOOK SEVEN: TWO TEMPTATIONS; CHAPTERS 63 - 71

CHAPTER SIXTY-THREE

Some of the townspeople, especially Reverend Farebrother, are aware that Lydgate is in financial difficulty. Lydgate prefers to keep his problems to himself, confiding in no one and asking assistance from no one (although Farebrother would be able to help him if he asked). It occurs to no one except Farebrother that Lydgate's marriage to Rosamond is not happy: she is becoming less attentive to her husband and to the problems she is creating for him.

Comment

The disparity between the illusion Lydgate creates for others and the disappointing reality of his marriage to Rosamond is the major focus of this chapter.

CHAPTER SIXTY-FOUR

Finally, Lydgate realizes that he must make a last plea to Rosamond to be more economical in her way of life. Spoiled and childish, she begins to cry and refuses to change anything. In fact, she even accuses him of stinginess. Her only suggestions are that they leave Middlemarch so that he can find a better paying position; they can also seek the help of his uncle, Sir Godwin. Lydgate tells her that he has planned to rent their house so that they will have more money. Stubbornly refusing to do as he wishes, she writes to Lydgate's uncle for help and also writes to the renting agent, advising that they have changed their plans about renting the house. She tells Lydgate of neither of these letters.

Lydgate's eventual discovery of what she has done fills him with anger and despair; yet he realizes that she will not change her habits-eventually he must ask his uncle, Sir Godwin, for help.

CHAPTER SIXTY-FIVE

One morning, a letter comes in the mail addressed to Dr. Tertius Lydgate. Rosamond notices that it is from Sir Godwin. Lydgate opens it and reads that his uncle is "not likely to have cash to spare." Lydgate accuses Rosamond of meddling; she accuses him of mistreating her, saying that it is she who has been wronged. Because he is kind-hearted and loves her, Lydgate again forgives her and even apologizes for his behavior. He tells her he realizes their situation is "ten times harder for her."

CHAPTER SIXTY-SIX

Lydgate, because of his anxiety about his present financial state, is unable to sustain any research or serious thought. At one time, he had resorted to the use of opium for temporary relief of mental strain; he had also tried alcohol and gambling, but they had never become a habit with him. He now feels that he must think of some means to raise some money to pay his debts. He believes that gambling is one way to win money quickly.

Lydgate meets Bambridge at the Green Dragon to discuss a horse that the latter was selling for him. While waiting for Bambridge, Lydgate plays a game of billiards; he begins to win and is covered by many bets. Fred Vincy and a friend, Hawley, arrive. Fred has been coming to the Green Dragon for several months to play and to converse with "men of pleasure" who frequent the tavern. He keeps a few pounds from his pay to wager if necessary. The last person he had expected to see was his stuffy brother-in-law, Dr. Lydgate, who is now playing as if his life depended on the outcome of the game. Young Hawley is beginning to get the best of Lydgate. Fred is in a dilemma as to what he should do to get Lydgate away from the game. He finally tells him that Reverend Farebrother is waiting to see him. This is enough to make Lydgate leave.

Later, Reverend Farebrother speaks to Fred, warning him that he will lose any chance of winning Mary if he should resort to his old ways of gambling. Fred realizes what a brave effort it was on the part of Farebrother to speak to Mary for him since he also loves her; at that moment he vows never to enter the Green Dragon again and to work harder to prove himself.

CHAPTER SIXTY-SEVEN

Since Sir Godwin has refused to assist Lydgate in his difficulties, the doctor unwillingly comes to the conclusion that there is no one for him to turn to but Mr. Bulstrode. He hesitates because of his dislike for Bulstrode. He receives a note from the banker: he wants to consult Lydgate at the bank about his "complaints." (Bulstrode has a tendency towards "hypochondria," or imaginary illnesses.)

Lydgate plans to use this opportunity to ask for a loan. Bulstrode is unsympathetic, because he has his own problems now with John Raffles. He coldly advises Lydgate to declare himself bankrupt. The banker then tells Lydgate that he has been considering leaving Middlemarch and transferring the management of the hospital to Dorothea, who is now a wealthy woman.

Comment

By leaving Middlemarch, Bulstrode hopes to avoid any scandal about his past should Raffles decide to talk.

CHAPTER SIXTY-EIGHT

On Christmas Eve, Raffles again visits Bulstrode, who has told his wife that he is "simply taking care of this wretched creature, the victim of vice, who might otherwise injure himself." He calls for a carriage for Raffles and warns him that he will pay him money only if he remains away from Middlemarch. If he returns, there will be no money for him.

Despite this uncomfortable arrangement with Raffles, Bulstrode senses that the only sure way for him to avoid a scandal is to leave Middlemarch. He asks the manager of his estate, Caleb Garth, to find a tenant for his house at Stone Court. Mr. Garth's first thought for manager of the property is Fred Vincy.

Comment

We can see that Mr. Garth's deeper purpose in asking Bulstrode to appoint Fred as manager at Stone Court lies in the hope that a responsible position will make Fred a reliable person, one whom his daughter could then be permitted to marry.

CHAPTER SIXTY-NINE

Caleb Garth rushes into the room where Lydgate is speaking to Mr. Bulstrode to tell him that he has found a man lying in the road. It is John Raffles; he is gravely ill and is calling for a doctor. Bulstrode is stunned; Caleb then reveals to Bulstrode that he knows of his past, because Raffles has told him. Caleb quickly offers to resign from his position as manager of Bulstrode's estate.

Lydgate examines Raffles and diagnoses his ailment as alcohol poisoning. He prescribes medicine and advises Bulstrode (who has wished for Raffle's death) that Raffles is to have no more alcohol.

Lydgate, returning home to face his own problems, sees his creditors removing some of his furniture because he has not been able to pay for it. Rosamond is noticeably shaken.

CHAPTER SEVENTY

Bulstrode is determined to keep a constant watch over Raffles so that no one other than Caleb Garth will learn about his past life. He begins to think he was hasty in his refusal of a loan to Lydgate. The doctor pays a visit to Raffles and prescribes extremely moderate doses of opium in case of sleeplessness. Before Lydgate leaves, Bulstrode presents him with a check for one thousand pounds.

Comment

Bulstrode has quickly become obsessed with the hope of Raffle's death, although he still maintains his good intentions of keeping him alive.

At six o'clock that evening, Bulstrode begins administering small doses of opium to the restless Raffles. Later in the night, he turns the care of Raffles over to his housekeeper, Mrs. Abel. He "forgets" to tell her when the medication should stop. Raffles dies the next morning but no one questions the circumstances of his death.

Comment

The question of Bulstrode's guilt for Raffles' death is debatable. Eliot presents the act as a moral transgression rather than a legal one.

CHAPTER SEVENTY-ONE

The scene is the Green Dragon tavern, where the men of the Middlemarch meet to drink and gossip. Mr. Bambridge, the horse dealer, upon hearing of the death of Raffles, reveals his own conversation with the dead man a few days before his death. Bulstrode's secret marriage and the truth about Will Ladislaw are made known, much to the consternation of those assembled. If Raffles knew Bulstrode's secret, is it not suspicious that he died in Bulstrode's home? Is it not also true that Dr. Lydgate, who attended the deceased, has been able to clear his numerous debts within five days of the funeral?

Before long, rumors fill the town of Middlemarch. Caleb Garth tells Bulstrode that he cannot be happy working for him and resigns his position. At a meeting to discuss medical procedures to be taken against the threat of a cholera epidemic, Mr. Hawley boldly demands that Bulstrode defend himself against Raffles' allegations. Bulstrode is frightened, but angrily attacks the "proceedings" against him. Physically and emotionally distressed, he needs assistance from Lydgate when he leaves. The doctor senses that Bulstrode's gift to him probably looks to others as if it was a bribe-perhaps, he thinks, it was.

Dorothea remains loyal to Lydgate. She tells Mr. Farebrother: "You don't believe that Dr. Lydgate is guilty of anything base? I will not believe it."

MIDDLEMARCH

TEXTUAL ANALYSIS

BOOK EIGHT: SUNSET AND SUNRISE; CHAPTERS 72 - FINALE

CHAPTER SEVENTY-TWO

Mr. Farebrother thinks there are no grounds to open a formal investigation to prove Lydgate guiltless; he does not relish the thought of asking Lydgate directly, since he has already seen some of the doctor's pride. Dorothea is annoyed with the Reverend for his unreadiness to defend Lydgate and advances a maxim: "What do we live for, if it is not to make life less difficult for each other?"

All the townspeople who know Lydgate are anxious to prove his innocence in the matter of Raffles' death. However, the circumstances surrounding the death leave them somewhat confused and uncertain about his motives. Dorothea is firmly convinced of his innocence, but she does not wish to confront him directly about the matter. Sir James thinks, "He must act for himself." Mr. Brooke is not sure of his innocence and wishes to avoid involvement because it will cost him money. Since Bulstrode has transferred the management of the New Hospital to Dorothea and she does have certain questions to ask Lydgate about it, she sees in this an opportunity to question him indirectly about Raffles' death.

Comment

Dorothea, an idealist like Lydgate, can readily appreciate the obstacles which beset one's plans to render service to others. Lydgate has lost both time and reputation because of his marriage to the prodigal Rosamond Vincy and the death of Raffles and the attendant guilt by association with Bulstrode.

CHAPTER SEVENTY-THREE

Lydgate himself is ready "to curse the day" he came to Middlemarch. His marriage is not the success he had hoped for; now his reputation is at stake because of Raffles and Bulstrode. He wants to clear himself but does not wish to implicate Bulstrode, especially if he is innocent, because he is now indebted to Bulstrode for the thousand pounds received the night before Raffles' death. Yet he decides to tell Rosamond nothing: "I shall do as I think right, and explain to nobody."

CHAPTER SEVENTY-FOUR

Because Middlemarch is a small town, "candor" is the vehicle used invalidly as an excuse to spread rumor. Inevitably, Rosamond Lydgate and Mrs. Bulstrode hear the stories about their husbands. Mrs. Bulstrode, who is liked and pitied by

Middlemarch wives, is deeply perturbed. Rosamond, on the other hand, is more severely criticized but is still thought to be merely the victim of a marriage to a stranger and interloper, since the Vincys are of old stock and solid reputation.

Mrs. Bulstrode has believed in her husband implicitly and is shaken when Mrs. Hackbutt hints that her friends will be "loyal" to her. She is unable to obtain any information until her brother, Mr. Vincy, tells her everything he knows. Harriet Bulstrode cannot forgive her husband and judges him harshly, since she had believed the story Bulstrode told her about Raffles being a sick, helpless man whom he had befriended. Finally she confronts her husband. Both begin to cry: his confession is silent. She cannot say, "How much is only slander and false suspicion?" and he cannot say, "I am innocent."

CHAPTER SEVENTY-FIVE

Rosamond is completely involved with her own wishes and the gratification of them. She remains unchanged; she is grateful that the debts have been paid but she cannot feel any happier about the success of her marriage. She still thinks Ladislaw will eventually admire her more than Dorothea.

Comment

Eliot observes that Rosamond is one of those women who live much in the idea that each man they meet would have preferred them if the preference had not been hopeless.

Rosamond thinks that Will would have been a more suitable husband than Lydgate. She is happy when Lydgate receives a letter from Will stating that he will arrive in Middlemarch in a few days. Lydgate has become increasingly moody and inclined to silence. Rosamond plans a dinner party but all the invitations are declined. He father tells her everything and then suggests that Lydgate leave town. Rosamond thinks that no one could be in a worse situation than she. Refusing to display her emotions to anyone, she also remains silent. Lydgate finally learns that Rosamond knows all, but she still says nothing. He wants her to be loyal and help him restore his reputation. But Rosamond cannot sympathize or console him about his problems because of her selfishness. Her advice is simple: "Let us go to London."

CHAPTER SEVENTY-SIX

Dorothea questions Lydgate about the management of the New Hospital. He mentions that he has been thinking of leaving Middlemarch. She takes this opportunity to beg him to tell her the truth of the Raffles matter and, at this time, he proclaims his innocence. Dorothea believes his story, then tells him that she will do all within her power to clear his name. She even offers to repay his loan from Bulstrode. Lydgate hopes he will be able to convince Rosamond that he wishes to stay in Middlemarch, at least until the townspeople believe his innocence in the matter.

CHAPTER SEVENTY-SEVEN

The following day, Dorothea pays a visit to Rosamond to explain her plans about using her money to clear Lydgate's name of any scandal. She enters the drawing room; seated with his back toward her, speaking in a low voice to Rosamond, is Will Ladislaw. Seeing Dorothea, his eyes seem "to turn to marble." Although shaken, Dorothea says in a firm voice that she has come to leave a letter for Dr. Lydgate. This "letter" is a note for one thousand pounds for Bulstrode. Indignant after her expedition, but determined to clear Dr. Lydgate, she returns to Freshitt Hall where she is still living with Celia and Sir James.

CHAPTER SEVENTY-EIGHT

Rosamond and Will stand almost paralyzed with shock from their experience. Will flies into a rage; Rosamond is in misery. He leaves, feeling that any hope of a future with Dorothea is ruined. Rosamond, still concerned with her own feelings, retires to bed. When Lydgate returns home, he finds her there, weeping hysterically. He knows that Dorothea went to visit his wife that afternoon but he has no idea of what happened, or that Dorothea never spoke to Rosamond.

Comment

The illusions which Rosamond has carefully nurtured suddenly evaporate when Will Ladislaw angrily berates her for ruining his reputation with Dorothea.

CHAPTER SEVENTY-NINE

Lydgate does not ask Rosamond if Dorothea has called to visit, but when he sees her letter on the table in the drawing room, he knows she has been there. Will Ladislaw arrives; Lydgate tells him that Rosamond is ill. (He does not know that Will has visited earlier that day.) The topic of their conversation is the one most discussed in Middlemarch: Raffles' death. Will admits only that he has had an encounter with Raffles, but he makes no mention of Bulstrode's connection with him. When Lydgate tells Will that Dorothea is the only one who has come to his assistance, he notices a change in Will's face. Suddenly, he realizes that Dorothea is the reason for Will's return to Middlemarch. The two men are "pitying" each other, but both are very much interested in their own problems and their dim prospects for the future.

CHAPTER EIGHTY

Dorothea is invited to have dinner at Reverend Farebrother's house. She enjoys these visits because there is always something of interest to be said or done there. Farebrother is very active in his parish and performs outstanding service for his parishioners, old as well as young. Dorothea is glad to have something to do to take her mind off Will Ladislaw. When his name is mentioned during the conversation, her former anguish returns. She excuses herself on the pretense of being overtired. She cries herself to sleep and dreams of Will. She awakens in the dawn, refreshed and with her sense of the life's ideals in perspective. Dorothea again becomes concerned with the problem of Lydgate's marriage, so she decides to pay another visit to the trouble Lydgate household-to speak Rosamond.

CHAPTER EIGHTY-ONE

On her second visit, Dorothea meets Lydgate, who mentions his wife's illness and then tells Dorothea that he has accepted her check most humbly and gratefully. Rosamond consents to see Dorothea, but is at a loss as to the purpose of Mrs. Casaubon's visit. She feels inferior to Dorothea, who is Lydgate's benefactor and Ladislaw's idol; she feels that Dorothea will parade her advantage before her.

Their meeting becomes emotional. Dorothea's heart goes out to the helplessness of Rosamond, who has become aware that she has misjudged Dorothea's motives. Dorothea explains to Rosamond that she had come the previous day to tell her of her plans to clear Lydgate's name. Dorothea passionately pleads Lydgate's innocence. Rosamond begins to cry hysterically when Dorothea says to her, "How can we live and think that anyone has trouble-piercing trouble-and we could help them, and never try?" She then gently chides Rosamond for not allowing her husband to be open with her. She then gives her ideas on marriage, but becomes too emotional to finish. Rosamond, guessing the reason for her emotion to be her thoughts of Ladislaw, tells Dorothea that she was mistaken about what she saw yesterday. Rosamond explains that Will was actually declaring his love for Dorothea and rebuffing hers.

Comment

When her artifice and self-possession are forgotten, Rosamond is capable of genuine feeling. By admitting her failure to captivate Will Ladislaw she has renewed Dorothea's trust in her character.

CHAPTER EIGHTY-TWO

Will thinks he has no choice now but to leave Middlemarch again. His primary reason for returning had been to see Dorothea; now he feels that she will have nothing to do with him. On a visit to the Lydgate household, Rosamond slips Will a note at tea which tells him that she has explained the situation to Dorothea. Exhilarated at this news, Will hopes for a reconciliation with Dorothea.

CHAPTER EIGHTY-THREE

Dorothea is relieved after her conversion with Rosamond. On the second morning after her visit, Miss Henrietta Noble, an aunt of Reverend Farebrother, pays a visit to her at the request of Will Ladislaw. She says Will fears he has offended her and asks if he may see her for a few minutes. Dorothea agrees. When Will arrives, she tells him she is "glad" he came. They stand silently at first but finally they confess their love for one another. He tells her that he cannot marry her because of Casaubon's will, which stipulates that she will lose the remaining money if they marry. She tells him that she hates her wealth, but her heart will break if he leaves. They decide to marry within three weeks.

Comment

Dorothea is independently wealthy, aside from her inheritance of Casaubon's estate.

CHAPTER EIGHTY-FOUR

The Reform Bill has been defeated in the House of Lords and Reverend Cadwallader, who favored the creation of peers to push through the bill, is discussing the political ramifications of the day with the Chettams and Mrs. Cadwallader on the lawn of Freshitt Hall. Mr. Brooke approaches dejectedly. He reveals the news of Dorothea's intended marriage to Ladislaw. Sir James turns white with rage; "I should have called him out and shot him," he cries. Reverend Cadwallader addresses Sir James, "My dear fellow, we are rather apt to consider an act wrong because it is unpleasant to us." Mr. Brooke decides not to think evil of Will until he hears good reason for doing so. He thinks of him in terms of a "son," inheriting Tipton and Freshitt. Mrs. Cadwallader remarks that "his blood is a frightful mixture."

Celia goes to her sister to advise her against the marriage. Dorothea tells Celia she is going to London; after much discussion, Celia realizes that nothing will change her sister's decision to marry Will. She fears that she will never see Dorothea again, since Sir James will not visit London because of his hatred for Will Ladislaw.

CHAPTER EIGHTY-FIVE

Bulstrode still has not made a full confession of his past life to his wife. He decides that someday (when he is dying) he will "tell her all." Mrs. Bulstrode suggests that they make amends to the Lydgates, who are also leaving Middlemarch. Bulstrode knows, however, that the doctor will not accept anything from him. Mrs. Bulstrode also advises him to make Fred Vincy the manager of the property at Stone Court. (Caleb Garth had resigned after Raffles told him of Mr. Bulstrode's past.)

CHAPTER EIGHTY-SIX

Caleb Garth learns of Mr. Bulstrode's plan to make Fred Vincy the manager of Stone Court. He wants to be the first to tell his daughter Mary. She is sitting in the garden. He casually begins a conversation about Fred; although she admits her love for him, she observes, "We must wait for each other a long while." When he tells her the news, she is filled with joy and rushes to tell Fred, who is coming to the garden to visit her. Fred is surprised and delighted. He and Mary sit in the garden for a long time to discuss their future.

Comment

The novel ends at this chapter. However, because Eliot knew her readers would like to know "how everything worked out" for her characters, she adds a Finale, or final chapter of explanation.

FINALE

Mary and Fred Vincy had both a happy and successful marriage. He became a theoretical and practical farmer and won the admiration of the people of Middlemarch. They had three sons to bless their marriage.

Dr. Lydgate gained an excellent practice in the area surrounding London. He and Rosamond "adjusted" to one another, each accepting the strong and weak points of the other's personality. He was a successful man (although he considered himself a failure), and died at fifty, leaving Rosamond and their four children. Later, she married an elderly and wealthy physician.

Dorothea and Will were still bound together by their strong love. She never repented that she had given up her wealth for her marriage to Will. He continued to work for the reforms which he had begun when he was a youth.

Mr. Brooke continued to correspond with Dorothea and Will and invited them to the Grange. Dorothea wrote Celia of the news that she had a son. Sir James finally relented, visiting them so that Celia could see the child. In this way a reconciliation was brought about between the two families. Mr. Brooke lived to a ripe old age and Dorothea's son inherited his estate.

Sir James, however, always regarded Dorothea's marriage as a mistake. He disliked Will, but never showed it openly for Celia's sake. The feeling was reciprocated on Will's part.

Those who did not know Dorothea usually thought she could not have been "a nice woman" because she married a much older man and then, a year after his death, threw away her inheritance and married a man young enough to be her first husband's son. Dorothea, however, led an important if obscure life; her good acts had a diffused effect on those around her. "The growing of good in the world is partly dependent on unhistoric acts." Our life is not as bad for us as it might have been, owing to the number of people like Dorothea who led hidden lives and who rest in "unvisited tombs."

MIDDLEMARCH

CHARACTER ANALYSES

Dorothea Brooke (later Mrs. Casaubon, Mrs. Ladislaw)

The idealistic and intelligent "heroine" of the novel, whose character and high values enable her to surmount the difficulties which her disappointing first marriage brings. Her second marriage is to Will Ladislaw; unlike the first, it is happy since it is based on a realistic appraisal of her husband's personality and career. "Her mind was theoretic, and yearned by its nature after some lofty conception of the world which might frankly include the parish of Tipton and her own rule of conduct there; she was enamored of intensity and greatness, and rash in embracing whatever seemed to her to have those aspects; likely to seek martyrdom, to make retractions, and then to incur martyrdom after all in a quarter where she had not sought it" (Book 1, Chapter 1).

Celia Brooke

The younger sister of Dorothea. Less intense than her sister, she marries Sir James Chettam, who had originally courted her sister. "The rural opinion about the new young ladies, even among the cottagers, was generally in favor of Celia, as being so amiable and innocent-looking, while Miss Brooke's large eyes seemed, like her religion, too unusual and striking. Poor Dorothea! Compared with her, the innocent-looking Celia was knowing and worldly-wise" (Book 1, Chapter 1).

Mr. Arthur Brooke

The uncle of Dorothea and Celia, a sturdy English squire. "Their uncle, a man nearly sixty, of acquiescent temper, miscellaneous opinions, and uncertain vote. He had traveled in his younger years, and was held in this part of the county to have contracted a too rambling habit of mind. Mr. Brooke's conclusions were as difficult to predict as the weather: it was only safe to say that he would act with benevolent intentions, and that he would spend as little money as possible in carrying them out" (Book 1, Chapter 1).

Rev. Edward Casaubon

A pedantic scholar who marries Dorothea because he sees in her a companion and secretary. "I feed too much on the inward sources; I live too much with the dead. My mind is something like the ghost of an ancient, wandering about the world and trying mentally to construct it as it used to be, in spite of ruin and confusing changes" (Book 1, Chapter 1).

Will Ladislaw

The young, handsome relative of Mr. Casaubon whose artistic and literary skills make him suspect to the people of Middlemarch. He becomes editor of the town newspaper. "Genius, he held, is necessarily intolerant of fetters: on the one hand it must have the utmost play for its spontaneity; on the other, it may confidently await those messages from the universe which summon it to its peculiar work, only placing itself in an attitudes of receptivity towards all sublime chances. The attitudes of receptivity are various, and Will had sincerely tried many of them" (Book 1, Chapter 10).

Dr. Tertius Lydgate

The "hero" of the novel is a medical man whose ideals and visionary plans are dimmed by the reality of a marriage to the selfish Rosamond Vincy. "He was but seven-and-twenty, an age at which many men are not quite common-at which they are hopeful of achievement, resolute in avoidance, thinking that Mammon shall never put a bit in their mouths and get astride their backs, but rather that Mammon, if they have anything to do with him, shall draw their chariot . . ." (Book 2, Chapter 15). "He carried to his studies in London, Edinburgh, and Paris, the conviction that the medical profession as it might be was the finest in the world; presenting the most perfect interchange between science and art; offering the most direct alliance between intellectual conquest and the social good" (Book 2, Chapter 15).

Rosamond Vincy

The beautiful, egotistical, and unrealistic daughter of the mayor of Middlemarch; the debutante who becomes the wife of Dr. Lydgate. "She judged of her own symptoms as those of awakening love, and she held it still more natural that Mr. Lydgate should have fallen in love at first sight of her. These things happened so often at balls, and why not by the morning light, when the complexion showed all the better for it? . . . And here was Mr. Lydgate suddenly corresponding to her ideal, being altogether foreign to Middlemarch, carrying a certain air of distinction congruous with good family, and possessing connections which offered vistas of that middle-class heaven, rank: a man of talent, also, whom it would be especially delightful to enslave" (Book 1, Chapter 12).

Fred Vincy

Rosamond's young, careless brother whose debts and lack of purpose prevent him from marrying his love, Mary Garth.

Mary Garth

The plain and practical daughter of the estate agent, Caleb Garth, who insists that Fred Vincy prove his stability before their marriage.

Mr. Vincy

The ambitious mayor of Middlemarch, whose indulgent attitude towards his son abruptly ends when Fred fails to receive a legacy from Peter Featherstone, his uncle.

Mrs. Vincy

Mother of Fred and Rosamond, she reflects an intense enjoyment of life, which may account for Fred's lack of direction and Rosamond's liberality.

Caleb Garth

The industrious, respectable, and charitable estate manager who often lends his time, skill, and money to others, even at the subsequent expense of his own family.

Nicholas Bulstrode

A strong, influential banker who suddenly discovers that his past life may be revealed and his reputation in Middlemarch destroyed.

John Raffles

The coarse, unscrupulous stranger who uses his knowledge of Will Ladislaw's and Mr. Bulstrode's pasts to make money by blackmailing Bulstrode. His subsequent death leads to a crisis in the lives of Bulstrode and Dr. Lydgate.

Joshua Rigg

The "frog-faced" man who becomes the heir to the land and fortune of Peter Featherstone; he is his natural son.

Peter Featherstone

The ailing, suspicious, and ill-tempered owner of Stone Court, a wealthy estate. The first of his two wives was a Garth; the second, a sister of Mrs. Vincy. His expected death leads to speculation about his legacy and becomes a focal point of interest in Middlemarch.

Reverend Camden Farebrother

The amiable and gifted vicar of St. Botolph's, who amends his minor vices when given the chance to assume the post of vicar of Lowick.

Mrs. Cadwallader

The wife of the rector of the parishes of Tipton and Freshitt, she is a lively hearer and teller of Middlemarch rumor. Of "immeasurably" high birth, she is not above stooping to matchmaking.

Sir James Chettam

The rejected suitor of Dorothea Brooke who finds a full and happy life when he marries her younger sister Celia.

MIDDLEMARCH

CRITICAL COMMENTARY

SENSE OF ORGANIC WHOLE AND SKILL IN PLOT

The attitude of many critics in the twentieth century to Victorian literature has been a mixture of indifference and contempt because of the marked impact of Freudian and Jungian psychological theory, the watersheds of two world wars, and the influence of Marxist philosophy. Yet for those who actually read the words of Dickens, Thackeray, and their contemporaries, the experience is rewarding. Apart from other considerations, these novelists and, in particular, George Eliot, were accomplished storytellers. Narrative, even in the stream-of-consciousness technique, involves incident; the mode and quality of the action create the interest, suspense, and surprise which characterize successful fiction. And here, in plot, is precisely where one finds the key to success in Eliot's novels. As Lord David Cecil has observed in *Early Victorian Novelists:* "It is very rare for a Victorian novelist before George Eliot to conceive the story as an organic whole of which every incident and character forms a contributory and integral part." The realistic quality of major incidents places no excessive burden upon the reader's credulity. Since what happens is probable, our suspension of disbelief is not impaired, for the motives and events which are presented to us in the action are justifiable and logical within the story's realm.

PERCEPTION OF PROVINCIAL ATTITUDES

Although George Eliot's technical skill is, perhaps, related chiefly to structural aspects, understanding and unraveling basic motivations found in human action are vital to her work. Claude Bisell (*ELH*, VIII) suggests that "George Eliot is at her strongest and best working in a social setting that she thoroughly understands and exploring a complicated network of motives with assurance and precision." The tracing of the thought of a character before he acts is a favorite interest of Eliot. The elaborate thought labyrinths of Henry James's characters are found only in Eliot's "aristocratic" characters (of whom there are relatively few in her novels). She is most accomplished, however, in explication of the thinking of the types that she understood best: the sturdy, respectable middle class and less complex lower classes of the era in which she lived. Years of extended observation and experience in Warwickshire and Coventry with the kind of people who inhabit her novels are reflected continually. Her preference is for unobtrusive picturing of the details of a character's thinking. Her use of the dramatic is very sparing and effective; it is employed primarily in scenes of conflict, such as those in which Dr. Lydgate and Rosamond or Raffles and Bulstrode engage.

PICTORIAL POWER MORE THAN DRAMATIC

Discussing the need for the dramatic in *The Craft of Fiction*, Percy Lubbock has noted: "Inevitably as the plot thickens and the climax approaches-inevitably, whenever an impression is to be emphasized and driven home-narration gives place to enactment. . . . Most novelists, I think, seem to betray, like Thackeray, a preference for one method or the other, for picture or for drama; one sees in a moment how Fielding, Balzac, George Eliot incline to the first, in their diverse manners, and Tolstoy (certainly Tolstoy, in spite of his big range) or Dostoevsky to the second, the scenic way."

PROBABLE INFLUENCE OF BALZAC

The view that Eliot may have been influenced in her style by Balzac is perhaps valid since in an essay which appeared in *The Leader* for July 21, 1855 called "The Morality of Wilhelm Meister" she eulogized Balzac as "perhaps the most wonderful writer of fiction the world has ever seen." That she could hardly have permitted herself to imitate his naturalism, however, is forcefully underlined by her comment in the same article "he drags us by his magic force through scene after scene of unmitigated vice, till the effect of walking among the human carrion is a moral nausea."

ELIOT COMPARED WITH TOLSTOY

From the English critic F. R. Leavis [*The Great Tradition* (London, 1948, pp. 124-125) comes the strong statement of Eliot's superiority over the later Victorian novelists and a comparison of Eliot with Leo Tolstoy, the author of *War and Peace*: "I affirm my conviction that, by the side of George Eliot-and the comparison shouldn't be necessary-Meredith appears as a shallow exhibitionist . . . and Hardy, decent as he is, as a provincial manufacturer of gauche and heavy fictions that sometimes have corresponding value. For a positive indication of her place and quality, I think of a Russian, not Turgenev, but a far greater, Tolstoy-who, we all know, is pre-eminent in getting the 'spirit of life itself.' George Eliot, of course, is not so transcendentally great as Tolstoy, but she is great, and great in the same way....Of George Eliot it can be said that her best work has a Tolstoyan depth and reality."

RATIONALISM AS HER "RELIGION"

Eliot's religious belief or lack of it is a topic which has brought forth divergent critical interpretations of her novels and correspondence. In his book *Nineteenth Century Studies*, Basil Willey, the respected English critic and scholar, disagrees with Lord David Cecil's view that George Eliot was "not religious." Willey fails to see why this expression is used by Cecil: "Religious," Willey states, "seems to me to be just what she was and many others of whom she is the type; the whole predicament she represents was that of the religious temperament cut off... from the traditional objects of veneration, and the traditional intellectual formulations." Although Eliot was not a "practicing Christian," Willey suggests that she knew "the hunger and thirst" for just living and the need for self-control and renunciation, "the need to lose one's life in order to gain it."

Jerome Thale, in *The Novels of George Eliot*, views the route of the Victorian intellectual-"extending from earnest belief through disbelief to a new, often secular, faith. As psychologist and as student of the new theology, George Eliot saw religion as valid subjectively rather than objectively. For her, our creeds, out notions of God, are true not as facts but as symbols, as expressions of states of mind. Faith is good as disbelief is bad, not because a God exists but because they are symptoms of a healthy state of consciousness. The novel does not give statements as explicit as this, but that is surely the inference to be made from the action."

A strikingly personal revelation of her view of man's need for religious belief occurs in a letter to Mme. Bodichon on November 26, 1862. "Pray don't ever ask me again not to rob a man of his religious belief, as if you thought my mind tended to such a robbery. I have too profound a conviction of the efficacy that lies in all sincere faith, and the spiritual blight that comes with no faith, to have any negative propagandism in me. In fact, I have very little sympathy with Freethinkers as a class, and have lost all interest in mere antagonism to religious doctrines. I care only to know, if possible, the lasting meaning that lies in all religious doctrine from the beginning till now."

ELIOT LETTERS ABOUT MIDDLEMARCH

December 1, 1871. "This day the first part of "Middlemarch" was published. I ought by this time to have finished the fourth part, but an illness which began soon after our return from Haslemere has robbed me of two months."

December 20 (Journal). "My health has become very troublesome during the last three weeks, and I can get on but tardily. Even now I am but on p. 227 on my fourth part."

January 29, 1872 (Journal). "It is now the last day but one of January. I have finished the fourth part-i.e., the second volume-of *Middlemarch*. The first part, published on December 1, has been excellently well received; and the second part will be published the day after to-morrow."

February 21, 1872 (Letter). "It has caused me some uneasiness that the third part is two sheets less than the first. But Mr. Lewes insisted that the death of old Featherstone was the right point to pause at; and he cites your approbation of the part as a proof that effectiveness is secured in spite of diminished quantity."

September 13, 1872 (Letter). "*Middlemarch* is done-all except a small finale, which I prefer reserving a little. The rest I hope to see the last little proof of at the beginning of next week."

November 4, 1872 (Letter). "I have finished my book [*Middlemarch*], and am thoroughly at peace about it-not because I am convinced of its perfection, but because I have lived to give out what it was in me to give, and have not been hindered by illness or death from making my work a whole, such as it is."

November 22, 1872 (Letter). "Except to be immensely disappointed with the close of *Middlemarch*. But look back to the Prelude."

December 1, 1872 (Letter). "... Maga's [*Blackwood Magazine's*] review of *Middlemarch*. I have just now been reading the review myself-Mr. Lewes had meant at first to follow his rule of not allowing me to see what is written about myself-and I am pleased to find the right moral note struck everywhere, both in remark and quotation. Especially I am pleased with the writer's sensibility to the pathos in Mr. Casaubon's character and position, and with the discernment he shows about Bulstrode. But it is a perilous matter to approve the praise which is given to our own matters."

ELIOT'S REPUTATION BASED ON HER PSYCHOLOGICAL INSIGHT

Because of the advances made in fiction techniques, and new scientific knowledge of the human psyche, the twentieth-century novelist has at his disposal much direction which George Eliot did not receive. Because their hasty and dilettante tastes prevent many readers and critics from even reading her novels (one supposes because of the didacticism of occasional chapters and a mistaken view that stereotyped sentimentality drips from every page), the real nature of her style and value remains relatively unknown to the general reading public.

Eliot's brilliant psychological penetration was one of the English models for which Proust admitted great admiration. The quality novels of Woolf, Joyce, and Faulkner and a handful of European novelists represent the best, in terms of technical advances and plumbing of the mind, that the twentieth century has produced. For her time, George Eliot's contributions both for virtuosity in form and in psychological depth are unmatched in English fiction.

MIDDLEMARCH

ESSAY QUESTIONS AND ANSWERS

Question: Who are the major characters in *Middlemarch* and what do they represent?

Answer: The most important portraits in this extensive gallery of English life are of two idealistic people: Dorothea Brooke (Mrs. Casaubon) and Dr. Tertius Lydgate. Both are intelligent, scrupulous, and dedicated to the task of improving the lot of their fellow men. He wishes to succeed in a far-reaching experiment and to broaden the effectiveness of the country hospital. She is concerned with improving the living conditions of poorer working classes by advocating the construction of modest cottages. Both visionaries, however, quickly find that ideas and ideals are, in themselves, no assurance of success. The way of the world is strong; complex obstacles appear to obstruct the best-intentioned plans. Human avarice, pettiness, or plain perverseness block progress. At times, their own romantic or injudicious make progress difficult. The marriages of Dorothea (her first) and Lydgate push them farther away from their broad humanitarian goals. Perhaps, then, a chief concern of the novel is to present two thoughtful, sensitive, but fallible people who are forced continually to sustain their strength in the realities of living.

Other characters in the novel represent various levels of English society at the time of the Reform Bill: Sir James Chettam and Mr. Brooke are typical of the wealthy, landed gentry; among the clergy Reverend Casaubon and Reverend Cadwallader are clearly a few rungs higher on social and economic ladders than Mr. Farebrother; Mr. Vincy and Mr. Bulstrode are, respectively, the mayor and the banker of Middlemarch, positions which give their families the opportunities for educational and cultural pursuits denied the less prosperous working families such as Caleb Garth's. Even on the lower social levels Eliot makes distinctions in rank among Trumbull the auctioneer, Bambridge the horse dealer, and dozens of minor characters who help to give the novel its panoramic effects.

Question: Why is *Middlemarch* considered one of George Eliot's best novels?

Answer: The book is representative of the most significant contributions which George Eliot made in English literature and in the development of the novel. First, it presents a vivid and accurate panorama of English life in the third decade of the nineteenth century. Readers such as William Wordsworth agreed that the pictures of rural people were authentic; from the wealthier class of squires and managers, down through the middle-class pictures of clergymen and professionals, to the simple farmers and journeymen, there is an unmistakable truth in her description and psychology. Her scenes of provincial life: the horse fair, the auction, the political rally, the hospital board meeting, the tavern gossip, the talk of workingmen, doctors, and clergy-all help to recreate an era with authentic color and movement.

Secondly, the complexity of the plot interests the reader consistently; skillful suspension of decision, which many characters face, stimulates curiosity; the abrupt revelation of sudden or hidden incidents creates surprise and intensifies interest. Some of the chief decisions made early in the novel include:

1. Dorothea Brooke's acceptance of Rev. Casaubon's marriage proposal.

2. Lydgate's choice of Rosamond as a wife.

3. Peter Featherstone's changing of his will.

4. Lydgate's vote for Mr. Tyke.

Thirdly, a mastery of deftness in characterization makes the reader interested in the future of most of the characters. Rarely are we unable to perceive a distinct human being made unique through specific details of speech, outlook, or action. Eliot's gifted insight into human motivation is apparent throughout; the characters act according to their natures after consideration of their choices: both Dorothea Brooke and John Raffles, for example, act the way we are led to believe they will act. The effective use of dialogue, suggestive **imagery**, autobiographical, ethical, and technical considerations also contribute to make *Middlemarch* a most valuable and artistic novel.

Question: Why is the book called "a novel about marriage?"

Answer: As in any novel, each of the four plots in *Middlemarch* is concerned with the problems which people face either because of circumstances or their own injudicious acts. Much of the action in each plot, however, is concerned with marriage difficulties.

a. Dorothea Brooke has romantically imagined marriage to Casaubon as a chance for her to fulfill an ambition to serve a great man in his work. Her illusions disappear, however, within a few weeks; even on her honeymoon in Rome she must face the sobering reality that her scholar husband married her for practical purposes, and is incapable of responding to her "ardent" nature. That she decides to remain loyal to him in spite of his shortcomings is, unquestionably, a difficult-even a noble-choice for her to make, considering how little joy she expects to receive in return from Casaubon.

b. Dr. Lydgate and Rosamond Vincy, like Dorothea Brooke and the Reverend Casaubon, have married for the wrong reasons. Rosamond's "theory" of love is that proximity breeds love; since Dr. Lydgate has to visit the Vincy household frequently owing to her brother Fred's illness, Rosamond presumes that they have fallen in love. To her, Lydgate fulfills her superficial requirements for marriage: he has the education, position, manners, dress, and voice she admires; in other words, all the external necessities needed to fulfill her concept of "husband." Indifferent and unconcerned about Lydgate's ideals, she later creates a burden of debt for him through her excessive and irresponsible spending. Lydgate, who had viewed his relationship with Rosamond merely as a harmless flirtation not to be taken seriously (because of his career plans), is moved by her tears; the sight of this single display of genuine emotion prompts him to ask for her hands. His life with Rosamond will be devoid of research and full of regret.

c. Mr. Bulstrode the banker and his wife Harriet have led a life together in which the real character of Bulstrode and his unscrupulous past have been concealed. His hypocrisy is finally revealed after the death of John Raffles.

    d. Mary Garth finds herself unable to accept Fred Vincy as a husband because of his careless, uncertain future. Unsure of a career and given to incurring gambling debts, Fred is able, finally, to correct his debilitating habits and to win her. Mary's common sense and realistic values prevent her from consenting to a marriage which promises little security. Unlike the other characters in the novel, who marry not for love but for some romantically specious reason, Mary is in love with Fred but refuses to risk union with him until she can be assured that he is capable of providing for a family.

Question: How is the term "The Wise Woman" used in reference to the novel?

Answer: George Eliot, like many Victorian novelists, often interrupts her story to comment on the significance of a character's thought or action. These omniscient observations are recognized by most critics as an explanatory or **didactic** technique, one not unlike the chanting of a chorus in Greek drama. The phrase "The Wise Woman" refers then, to the voice of the author. It is usually heard at the end of the chapter Leavis and Quentin Anderson agree in their detection of a personal tone in Eliot's comparison of Dorothea to a saint. In the Prelude Eliot says: Here and there is born a Saint Theresa, foundress of nothing whose loving heartbeats and sobs after an unattained goodness tremble off and are dispersed among high instances, instead of centering in some long recognizable deed." Whether Eliot's comments enhance the novel's art or not is a choice left to the reader's judgment.

Question: What are the dominant images in the novel?

Answer: By using carefully chosen **imagery** Eliots has intensified emotional aspects of characters and given insights into the planning of her novel's structure. Casaubon's life, for example, is usually described in terms of small, confining places. His rooms are dark, stuffy, and old. He reveals in one of his first speeches that he keeps part of his research materials in "pigeon-holes." He is reminiscent of a "specimen from a mine" or "a description above the door of a museum."

The novel is a complex one, and Eliot has been required to weave together strands of several plots, each of which contains characters whose lives intersect with others. As Professor Gordon S. Haight has pointed out, there are numerous images of weaving, binding, and linking in *Middlemarch:* "Some of them refer to Lydgate and Rosamond. Lydgate has set out to discover the tissue common to all living matter, taking up the thread of his investigations or adding links to the chain of scientific evidence; but he is caught in the gossamer web of love, and his life is bound into one with Rosamond's. From the beginning she has woven a little future for herself. When she lays aside her reticule she is seldom without a thread in her hand for lace-making or tatting."

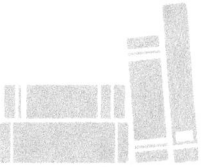

BIBLIOGRAPHY

The complete *Works of George Eliot* has been published in twenty-five volumes (Warwickshire edition, 1908). Following is a list of titles under two general topics. Plentiful material concerning *Silas Marner* and *Middlemarch* may be found in the works listed.

LETTERS

Haight, G. S. (ed.) *The George Eliot Letters.* 7 vols.

BIOGRAPHY

Cross, J. W. George Eliot's Life as Related in her Letters and Journals. *3 vols.* (1885)

Hanson, L. and E. M. *Marian Evans and George Eliot.* (1952)

Stevens, George. George Eliot. *(1902)*

Haldane, E. S. George Eliot and her Times. *(1927)*

May, J. Lewis. *George Eliot; a Study.* (1930)

Bullett, Gerald. George Eliot: Her Life and Books. *(1947)*

Williams, Blanche C. *George Eliot: A Biography*. (1936)

CRITICISM

Thale, Jerome. The Novels of George Eliot. *(1959)*

Stump, Reva. Movement and Vision in George Eliot's Novels. *(1959)*

Bennett, Joan. George Eliot: Her Mind and Art. *(1948)*

INDIVIDUAL CHAPTERS OF CRITICISM

Woolf, Virginia. *The Common Reader*. (1925)

Cecil, Lord David. *Early Victorian Novelists*. (1935)

Leavis, F. R. *The Great Tradition*. (1948)

Baugh, Albert C. and others. *A Literary History of England*. (1948)

Stevenson, Lionel. *The English Novel*. (1960)

Baker, Ernest. *The English Novel*. Vols. III, IV. (1930, 1934)

www.ingramcontent.com/pod-product-compliance
Lightning Source LLC
LaVergne TN
LVHW021701060526
838200LV00050B/2460